"Joe Conniff's book is a tour-de-force; a page-turner that doesn't portray the writer as a beast of burdens, but lays bare the deep emotional scars within the soul of addicts everywhere. Exploring his inconvenient truths and unlocking the complex despair that misleads any person down a path of drugs and addiction is tough to read and stomach, but as a writer and recovery coach, Joe knows that. He forces the audience to take an unflinching look at an all too familiar story that's happening not only at drug markets across the concrete jungle... But behind the white picket fences of every suburb in America. This is a MUST READ for addicts, parents of addicts and those that's lives have been turned upside down by the opioid epidemic."

-Kevin Ronca, Producer of "Nightcrawlers"

"Conniff courageously guides readers through his personal story of addiction - from its early roots, to life on the streets, to the treatment model that would ultimately save his life. Causes and Conditions offers a critical lens into the core of what drives substance abuse – trauma, lack of support, emotional loneliness – while offering real, proven solutions for recovery. Conniff effectively moves back and forth in time, weaving his first-hand experiences with the wisdom he's gained along the way. This story of triumph and overcoming offers a beacon of hope to those who are

still struggling...and an approach to healing worthy of our attention."

-Cheryl Przezdziecki, Licensed Mental Health Counselor

"This book is a powerful public testament to Joe's vulnerability and authenticity, two qualities that I have deeply appreciated him sharing with me during my own process of becoming these past two years. By displaying courage in working through inventory and the amends process I have discovered the courage to do the same. The result has been my own personal transformation towards stability, humility, radical acceptance, and appreciation. This book contains powerful truths, and I know with first-hand knowledge that the truths Joe tells are backed by compassionate action and high regard for the potential in all of us."

-Wesley Dean Irwin, M.Ed.

Teacher/ Author of "The Adventures of Aleia" Series

Causes and Conditions

Causes and Conditions

A Life Experience in Addiction and Recovery

Joseph Conniff

Joseph Conniff

CONTENTS

CONTENTS

Foreword

There's an old Japanese koan, known as "Kyogen's person up a tree." An ordained person, wandering in unfamiliar mountains becomes lost. Tired and starving they come upon a tree. Gazing at the limbs that span out over a steep ravine, there appears to be fruit. Hoping to end their hunger, they climb onto a lone tree limb.

Almost to the fruit, a droplet of water strikes the limb. Then another, and another, and then a great gust of wind swept the person from the tree's limb. As they tumble, a branch strikes their mouth, and they bite down. Their hands and feet flailing cannot grab hold of the tree. Suddenly from below, they hear a bellowing voice with a question. "What is the meaning of Bodhidharma's coming from the West?" Eyebrows raised, they are in a terrible dilemma. Should they open their mouth to answer, they will fall to their death. If they do not answer the questioner, they will have failed their vow as an ordained. In such a circumstance, how should one answer?

I first met Joseph at Rebel Saints Meditation Society on Capitol Hill in Seattle, Washington. Though I've been in recovery for 33 years from active addiction, my big lesson has been that while our life's details can differ dramatically, the nature of who we are is the same. We are all fundamentally loving, caring, seamless presence AKA "Rebel Saints." Despite our sameness in nature, our ability to act on it is an entirely different story.

What I noticed about Joseph from the start was his straightforward and direct nature. There wasn't a wishy-washy, static retreat, or slick vibe with him. He didn't have a bunch of shit with him. What I saw was what I got. The merciful bonus was, he didn't feel like he was vibrating out of his body and doing that talking in circles like many of us do when we first come in. That's because we have no idea whether we're shot, screwed, or powder-burned for the first few months. Just because we stop getting high doesn't mean that we necessarily stop being toxic; physically, mentally, emotionally, and spiritually.

One of the truths that I've learned over the years is, just because you can tell your story to people doesn't mean that you necessarily understand it. In my experience, for it to have impact and meaning, there has to be something more than regurgitating facts, dates, times, places, and events. There's another dimension. We need to feel, deal, integrate, reconnect, and heal what I described earlier as our fundamental nature. That's not an easy or transactional process. It's one transformative one. It requires six basic elements, known as "Paramitas," or practice that lead to completeness. They are: 1) Generosity 2) Ethical conduct 3) Patience 4) Fortitude 5) One-pointed undivided stabilized Presence and 6) Wisdom.

Joseph's sharing embodies all six paramitas at a fantastic depth, not as an event but as an ongoing practice and unfolding process. A loving, caring, seamless presence that is capable of endless expansion. And this is the nature of Joseph's experience, and knowing his own story in a very intimate way, that isn't merely regurgitation. He was that person up a tree, as Zen master Kyogen described. He was dangling between life and death. He was caught in the high winds of addiction mind. He was that distorted sense of self that can't get out of one's own way. And despite his precarious circumstances, he found a way to answer the call in the wilderness, not failing his personal vow as a human being, and came down from the tree with a hunger that has been satisfied. Please enjoy his hard-won experience. It's 360° beautiful.

Rev. Seiho Mudo Morris
Mentor Garden Zendo, October 2020

Introduction

I remember thinking to myself many times, "I don't want to be an addict, I never asked for my life to be like this", as I laid out cardboard for bedding in the alleys of Seattle. It just wasn't something I planned. But I became one. Not knowingly, and not overnight; it happened gradually and progressively. I've come to understand that no one would willingly sign up for the type of life that an addict lives. It's a life familiar with pain, self-hatred, incarceration, trauma, and death.

By the time I began writing this, I'd personally known thirty to forty people to die from an overdose or drug-related death. Personally. Not a news story, not a friend of a friend, or something like that. From my years in high school, to my life experiences in five different states, or clients I've worked with in the last four years, these are all people that I had gotten to know, spent time or shared valuable moments of life with. Someone else's son or daughter, partner, or parent. Chances are, if you're reading this, you're also familiar with the experience. Maybe you've received that phone call; been there to identify a friend or family member, and attended the memorial service. Bought flowers, signed the card, shared photos and memories on social media. Perhaps you're a person in active addiction or recovery, and you question if you ever gave someone the dope that took their life, that's something I think about every day. I would wind up attending many drug-related funerals long before I became convinced my family might have to attend mine.

So if that's the case, if the addicted life wasn't my intention, what in the hell happened? How did I finally end up arrested for selling heroin to an undercover cop, living out of doors, a full-blown addict on the streets of Seattle? What makes someone throw away all things worthwhile in life for some short term pleasure? My addiction started roughly around age 16, and I got clean at 32. This book captures the better part of a 16 year drug addiction; all that led up to it and all that came with it; and five plus years of recovery.

If we are strictly valuing a person's time in sobriety in an effort to learn about and understand the nature of addiction and recovery, one may assume I know very little about living a life free from drugs and alcohol. But here's what I know, that's exactly how I want to live today; a life free from drug and alcohol addiction. And the cold, hard truth is, after all those years of using, I probably still know more about consuming and dealing drugs than I do about recovery. Honestly though, I consider that the twenty years I invested in both my use and recovery makes me rather well suited and qualified to be an expert on addiction and recovery as it pertains to my experience, in an unconventional but very practical manner. To be clear though, one can only be an expert on their own addiction/ recovery; as I can't be an expert on yours or someone else's. That's just not the way it works.

You should understand now that this is not a book about my "disease of addiction". It is about addiction, yes, but I will not refer to my own personal addiction as a disease. I don't ascribe to that model based on what I have experienced collectively in my adverse childhood experiences, substance use, recovery and healing practices utilizing peer led programs, meditation and mindfulness practices. The truth is, I learned my addiction like a human learns anything: repetitive action. I learned it as a response and attempt at relief to events in my life, both difficult and traumatic, and eventually it became the only life I would know for some time.

During that time I would endure significant difficulties with my mental health (MH), but hell, show me anyone who lives or has lived with addiction that hasn't endured some degree of depression, or experiences anxiety as a result of the prolonged ups and downs of substance use disorder (SUD). The good news for me is because of a establishing a process of recovery I've unlearned my addiction.

I do agree that SUD is a disease, and absolutely believe that medicalizing addiction as a disease has benefited individuals affected by it because it allows to secure ongoing funding, research and avail treatment to many who need it, yet I don't believe that I personally live with a disease. In my own journey, believing that I had the "disease of addiction" anchored me to programs and rooms for a period of time in which I was unable to understand the value of my own agency in overcoming my day to day experiences of the human condition.

The areas of this book where I emphasize what works for me in my recovery should be understood as the unlearning of my addiction to substances, and seen as a process of self-empowerment. I have some barriers to identifying with "being in recovery" due to the contemporary use and meaning of recovery, as I have not regained anything, nor did I previously know a normal state given the nature of my life growing up. I believe that "becoming" is more of what has happened to me since renouncing substances. But for the sake of this book and the perspectives in it, I will confine my conversations to my understanding as it relates to the words "addiction" and "recovery", since they are far more common and accepted in our communities and the world of behavioral health.

What I discuss in these pages has only been *my* experience. This book is not meant to be a source of verifiable solutions, nor is it meant to paint a picture of every addict walking among us; though I imagine many of the things covered here will resonate for some readers. Over the course of these pages I hope to shed some light on what drove this addict-alcoholic to the brink of self-destruction, and eventually, to find and live a life in recovery. My experience and process of overcoming my addiction is not intended to belittle anyone else's program, nor to devalue what the disease model has done to support the recovery of millions of others. Nothing I say in this book should be taken as an attack on what works for you or someone else. My sole intent is to expand the reader's understanding through a lens into my life in addiction, hoping one finds resonance and value to share with others in an effort to raise awareness and understanding.

Since many of the people I have met in the recovery process find different motivations and paths out of their addictions, the goal of my writing here is to push the reader into the spirit of engaging dialogue and supporting efforts to alleviate SUD within their own community. I hope that as you move through these pages, you can put aside any existing biases and formulate your own questions in an effort to better understand the nature of addiction and recovery. Remaining open to ideas and pathways allows us to have a better understanding of the causes and conditions that lead to addiction and recovery, with no expectation of learning how to fix someone by reading this book alone. Through the experience of reading my story, I want to encourage the reader to connect to the humanity in these pages; look for similarities and leave aside the differences. We need to let go of what we think we know about substance use disorder, and look at how we can become more aware in our personal understanding of socio-economic factors so we can affect change and heal our communities and loved ones. Not looking for fix all or blanket solutions gives us room to improve on what the whole individual needs. I've come to know that we can't fix everybody, or at least I can't; some individuals will require assistance in carrying the weight and trauma of their lives and some folx may never experience full abstinence, and that's ok.

In the final pages I will discuss my personal thoughts and ideas of solutions to decrease the impact and loosen the grip that addiction currently has on our nation. Based on my experience yet to unfold here, I would like to be clear that by no means do I believe we can arrest our way out of addiction/ SUD. I am not writing a book to direct your attention to the legal system as any type of solution in hopes that we resolve what I believe to be a deeply complex societal issue. Though overcoming my addiction involved an arrest and participation in a program administered through the criminal legal system, which you will hear about in detail, I would like to emphasize that because of my white privilege, the design of a therapeutic court and it's intervention did my access to resources, taking of suggestions and support from family and peers lead to long term recovery. So with that said, yes, that system did provide me with an exit from addiction, as it has for many others. It supported my goals and nurtured my process of recovery. Is it ideal for everyone? No. I believe the program that I participated in was therapeutic for my needs, but therapeutic is not the design or outcome of every diversion court program in existence. I don't believe that the criminal legal system can be relied upon to be consistently therapeutic, especially when the process of arrest and incarceration, so often the start of system involvement, are deeply distressing experiences. As mentioned, I believe SUD to be a societal issue, fraught with public health concerns and racial disparities that thrive on isolation, discomfort in the human experience, generational trauma, and an overall lack of biopsychosocial well-being; and none of these can be totally remedied through involvement in such a system as it currently exists in America.

It's important to acknowledge and educate ourselves about this nation's harmful policies, past and present, while dismantling systems of institutional racism, mass incarceration, militarized policing, and once and for all stop hoping that if we lock people up, the issues will go away. Radical changes in drug policy, addressing the role of judicial interventions and a complete overhaul of policing constitute an imperative slice of the pie in the aim of making more equitable pathways of recovery possible. Contemporary drug policies were initially shaped by the experience and biases of individuals and politics upholding a system of white supremacy, and have long since worn out their welcome. They've caused extensive damage including generational trauma to Black and brown communities, and furthered the desire for many members of our society to seek temporary relief in substances.

Another intention is to provide a vivid picture on what events took place in my personal life; to bring awareness to the impact of adverse childhood experiences and how I became a product of my environment. I will take you through my formative years, time in the military, my late 20's and early 30's, hand in hand with the progression of my addiction. All of this finally compounded with multiple arrests, treatment, resources, connection to a recovery community and finally developing true understanding; a willingness and desire to finally change the way I dealt with reality. Changing my addictive behaviors was never part of my plan. In many ways, it was afforded to me in white, cis-hetero, able-bodied male privilege; but most of all the unorthodox privilege of being addicted to drugs that would finally bring me to my knees on the streets of Seattle. I will describe in detail how my involvement in programs worked, from my perspective, and which of those resources positively impacted me, and how I carry this experience and wisdom to others still living with SUD. This book is about the causes and conditions of my addiction and recovery. I will share the impact of those I see still addicted in my community, those that inspired my recovery; my spiritual teachers; disciplines, practices and what was suggested by sponsors and mentors that encouraged me along the way. With that said, I have little interest in offering pages full of statistics and data in a time in which all the necessary research is readily available by experts in the fields; validating that we need to embrace multiple paths out of addiction, expand treatment and end the drug war.

For the next fifteen chapters you are going to get to know a drug addict, intimately; but don't stop here. Interview and get to know others with lived experience; hear their story, about what happened, and what was or is missing from their life. Hear their dreams and aspirations, what music they love, or what trade they have worked in. With that said, I sincerely hope the interviewee is not your partner, or child; but chances are, knowingly or unknowingly, we are all at arm's length from someone living with an SUD. This may also present a challenge; people have a tendency to distance themselves from those in addiction, not just because of the unpredictability of substance use and its volatility, but because we see our very own glaring addictive behaviors of escaping from reality.

Addiction is often rationalized and encouraged every day in American life. We have a culture of wine moms, pub crawls and t-shirts about the next inbound drink or happy hour. We are bombarded with advertisements of the newest electronics, trending fashion, or sporting event and which alcohol producing giant is sponsoring it. Many states have now decriminalized and legalized marijuana, and the signage jumps out at us up and down the freeways; meanwhile our attention is pulled away from the task of driving our vehicle into desiring the luxury sedan in the next lane over.

Look around while taking public transit; many of us are reaching for our devices; especially in a momentary sense of boredom or feeling of discomfort, moments when we feel vulnerable and should be reaching out in our skin to connect with other beings. Instead, we fake our connection through social media and online dating apps. We overindulge in unhealthy behaviors in front of the TV, or in the prepackaged food aisles at the grocery store and are still left wanting. We get a promotion at work, only to be left thinking about another advancement opportunity. We are left grasping at the next level of safety or security, much the way I thought about the next fix as soon as I had acquired the first. We wrestle with greed of that which brings pleasure, hatred of things that are carriers of pain or discomfort; and we are in deep delusional states that the activities and behaviors we partake in are actually helping us to smooth out the ride. Is a "normal" person really much different than the substance using individual? Many of us let any inkling of self-esteem be driven by the number of likes and followers on our Instagram accounts, and tend to value others based on those numbers and quality of reviews. Still left wanting is the addict alive in all of us; and this repetitive cycle of craving is at the core of all human existence.

Stemming from a phrase coined by Johann Hari in his popular TED Talk, some of the most revered people writing on or discussing addiction agree that the opposite of addiction is not sobriety; it's connection. Unfortunately, our society has been overrun with the notion that happiness and balance are only readily available materially, outside of ourselves and others; that it can be bought or found via the recently released medication or digital app. There are some organizations taking what does work out of the ability to connect in seconds through our fingertips with twelve step meeting searches by area and location on maps; recovery support applications and many other online forums for support and grounding in times of need. I find that to be one of the wisest uses of technology as of recent; yet I feel this is not the only kind of connection necessary to really make an impact on matters like the addiction crisis. Building on Hari's TED Talk, we need genuine human engagement and connection. The kind that gets us up close and personal, includes compassion and empathy, and shows us that we are more in this together than we are separate; we are interdependent. The hard fact is that many of us, middle class on down, are one or two paychecks away from a financial crisis that could land us out of doors, or one sports injury and a surgery away from developing an unstable relationship with prescription painkillers. In matters like these we are regularly reminded of the uncertainty of our human condition.

Recently, social media apps like Facebook and Nextdoor have become platforms for disgruntled residents of Seattle to address those living out of doors, many of which are struggling with SUD, barking about them like zoo or circus exhibits that won't perform as expected when we want them to. I agree that there are distressing amounts of property crimes associated with substance use disorder, and some argue that they have employed their compassion by voting on affordable housing and increased budgets for social services, yet that it has only enabled many to remain in addiction or homelessness; that the affected individuals don't really want to change. Is this truly the case? Is that actually compassion in action? Compassion is the act of understanding the human desire to be free from suffering. Even the person that breaks into my vehicle and steals from the local shop owner has the same longing for happiness and freedom from suffering that I do. Imagine that. I would think that the compassionate approach many blame for perpetuating addiction rather than helping to resolve it, is not the right kind, and actually not compassion at all. As if because one showed up and voted for affordable housing and expansive funding, that alone should have been enough to really uproot the issue they have to look at on their commute home. The true compassionate approach that is missing in many communities is that people need to understand that addiction does not discriminate, but our systems do. Addiction doesn't care about your skin color, how much money you have today or what job you might hold tomorrow, but those are the deep seated factors in who receives access to treatment rather than lengthy prison sentences; connection vs. further disconnection.

I have seen the needles in the parks and on sidewalks around our city. Today though, the most frustrating part about these sights is not so much that I have to explain a syringe on the ground to my child or encounter someone in a mental health crisis, but rather that someone's parent might die alone in the streets tonight. Somebody else won't get the same opportunity I did to recover and be a present parent. So if I have been afforded the opportunity to overcome my addiction, the question is: What can I do for those still caught up in their substance use?

Many of those discussions aforementioned on social platforms have led me to be vocal about my stance on these matters as a person in recovery, only to be written off, and told they're happy for me that I was able to help myself. If I was able to help myself, I wouldn't have been motivated to write this book. There would be nothing to write about, since other people would be helping themselves out of the pit of addiction. The reality is that I was unable to help myself. My community supported me and my peers held out hope; and people I didn't even know believed in me. As it's been said, it takes a village to raise a child right? Well, it's going to take the village to help raise our neighbors and loved ones up out of addiction.

So beyond these pages and my story, I also implore you to get to know others in recovery. The power and passion exemplified by those who have been to their brink of insanity and death, and lived to tell about it; those are some of today's truest heroes. We should be past the point of glorifying wars and soldiers abroad, when we have battlefields on our streets and in our homes trying to keep our communities and loved ones alive in the face of addiction. Many of our military veterans are dying in our streets displaced and often forgotten after their service, when substances provide a certain temporary relief from the horrors of wartime PTSD, grief and loss. Here in these pages you will get to know me, also a veteran.

My life in this book is not in chronological order, so you will read a chapter about more recent events, and the following two chapters will journey back about past experiences, and it will continue in that format until the events and timeline intersect. Though many names and certain identifying details have been changed to protect the privacy of individuals, you will read about my life experiences and those that have had impactful roles in it; but my story through words here might not be quite as impactful as if you find a member of your own community who has overcome their obstacles with substance use and has now turned that effort and energy that went into using, into something beautiful; into an existence with less pain and unnecessary suffering. We are your small business owners, artists, bus drivers, celebrities, public servants and officials, and we are so much more than who we are in our addictions, because we can and do recover.

My name is Joe; I'm 37 years old. I'm a father, spouse, son and a retired drug addict. And I'm fortunate to say that I've lived two lives in one lifetime, and am truly grateful to drugs and alcohol for that. This is my story.

1

Crosstown Traffic April 24th 2015

Down in Post Alley I could hear the sound of cars and metro buses thickening on the viaduct and streets above. It was shortly before 7 a.m. and the kitchen deliveries were starting to pull up on the cobblestone; before long they'd be kicking us off of the steps so they could gain access to the restaurants.

We had made our spot on the platform and steps late into the evening the night before, after the Pike Brewery closed. About this time in the morning the brushing and beeps of the sidewalk washing equipment had become harmonious up on First Avenue. For anybody in active addiction, those sounds were a friendly reminder of the most opportune time of the day to score and sell dope in downtown Seattle.

For many, this would be the time of the morning when the homeless along the backside of Macy's or some other downtown area had been moved on so businesses could open, and they would make their way to the Blade in hopes of scoring the first bag of the day. In my case, this could mean waiting around until some construction worker would make a stop downtown hoping to score a little black before heading off to their jobsite for the day; and for the right amount of money and knowing who was holding, I could get cut in for helping him score and get myself well.

The Blade exists as a small section of downtown Seattle, most notably between Pike and Pine Streets on Third Avenue, where open air drug dealing, use, retail theft and the fencing of stolen goods occurs, and I knew I had to get well before the dealers moved away from the downtown corridor for the afternoon. SPD had just spent the last two days sweeping boosters, dealers and users, and staying out here much past 9 a.m. was really asking to get picked up. The only reason we ended up down here at all is because Benny was out here to re-up at 10 p.m. and he was the only one with the audacity to be out on the Blade selling dope in the height of a task force bust. For me I didn't have a choice, I had been out of doors for four months and I went wherever the dope was; plain and simple.

I woke Sarah, and after folding up the cardboard we used as a buffer to the cement, we hit the market to fix in the restrooms below the arcade.

Sarah was a sex worker who had become a friend over the last nine months. We spent the previous night hustling little deals, trying to put together enough money to hit a cheap motel on 99 and clean up a bit. Until two days before, it had been a couple of months since we had caught up with each other. We used to crash up at old man Mark's on Aurora; he and I would move bags downtown while she'd walk the avenue for clients. Finally we'd all get together in the evening to lay back and get high. Our only goal for today though was to pool cash and dope and try again for a room up at the Oaktree Motel.

Sarah came out last and said, "Meet at Fred Meyer on 85th at 10 a.m.?"

"Sounds good to me." I told her, and she went up to Third Ave to catch the E-Line. I made about three hopeful laps around Third and Fourth between Pike and Pine Streets before deciding to move closer to Pacific Place and see who was coming down off the I-5 on ramp homeless camp.

As I made my way up to the Convention Center, I realized that the Seattle PD bike patrol had just gotten done waking the folx there and moving them along. I walked back towards the Columbia store and saw Mack coming at me with a beat up canvas bag.

Mack was a bigger light-skinned fella I'd buy rock from once in a while, and he was one of the regular dealers that stuck around Second Avenue. He had done some time on and off and was getting into pushing black here and there, but was easily involved in any other money making opportunities out on the Blade.

"Eh-yo....you know how to get these security tops off?" he asked.

He had about six or seven fifths of liquor that he had just knocked off from one of the stores near Belltown.

"Yeah, let's head down towards the Harbor Steps and I'll help you out." I said.

"Cool, cool....yeah I'll throw you a little something for your time. Hey, did you hear they just grabbed Big D first thing in the morning yesterday off the block? Caught him with a lot of dope."

"Yeah", I said, "They're coming down hard and quick out here, and a ton of people are dope-sick with nobody to score from."

The liquor bottles had the red anti-theft security tops still on, and if he stood any chance of making a few bucks off of them he needed them ready for consumption. Mack saw me flying a sign a week before and gave me a couple bags of black to get well, so I felt like I kind of owed him a little. We crossed the street towards Starbucks on Third by the Kress Market and headed south.

As soon as we put our feet on the curb, Mack gave me a nudge and said, "Man, that ride's get up looks like some kinda cop car."

Just as I looked up, the black Suburban shot diagonally across from the Bartell store. Before I could even take in what was happening, four cops jumped out and threw me against the window at Starbucks.

"Major Crimes Task Force. You're under arrest as a suspect in an ongoing narcotics investigation."

Well, shit. I didn't even really get well yet and here we go again. Right away I was forced face first against the wall next to Starbucks. They shook me down, ran my pockets, and cuffed me. First my bandana got ripped off, exposing my unkempt overgrown mess of hair, and then they pulled a crack pipe, sheet of black-tracked tinfoil and some empty baggies out of my outer jacket pocket.

As they turned me around, one of the officers showed me a picture and asked, "Do you know this guy?"

I shook my head no, chuckling to myself. Of course I knew him, everybody knows him. Everybody who does or sells anything out here knows each other. The man's picture was just one of many small time dealers with a goofy nickname supporting his habit, like most of us in the downtown corridor.

"Nope." I said.

As I looked around the Blade, it felt like there were 200 people watching me get bagged that morning. It was almost a perfect Seattle day in April, no showers, and the cozy PNW overcast and cool air was coming in off of Elliot Bay. Almost a perfect day; except I knew I was in a world of shit with this one. Narcotics investigation? I thought to myself, but how? I had only been selling to people I knew, addicts like me living out of doors down here. I mean everybody knew the sweep was coming, but I had been taught by the more seasoned street veterans how to avoid selling to the undercovers that had been out there. But then again, everyone seemed to be getting popped these last two days.

Mack grabbed his bag and said, "Y'all have a good day now!"

What the hell? Mack was carrying a bag full of liquor bottles that were clearly stolen but they handed his ID back to him, and southbound he went down Third Avenue.

Shit. Whatever they have on me must be pretty solid since they are just cutting him loose. Looks like I won't make that meeting with Sarah in Greenwood at 10 a.m. after all.

"Take him over to the West precinct, a whole bunch of them have already been picked up today." said one of the officers.

An SPD Ford Explorer had just rolled up. The back door opened, revealing the rock hard plastic seat that I'd become so familiar with this last year, followed by the words, "watch your head".

Fuck.

In January 2015, the Seattle Police Department and FBI began a concerted effort to combat the high level of crime occurring in the nine and one half block area surrounding Third Avenue between Pike and Pine St. In 2014, there were over ten thousand calls for police service in this area alone, which amounts to a staggering 27 calls per day. Four of the seven most dangerous blocks in the city fall within this area, as measured by the number of violent crimes. In 2014, 180 violent crimes occurred in this small area of Seattle. Over the course of the concerted operation, undercover officers conducted 177 transactions with 148 individuals, purchasing heroin, methamphetamine, cocaine, pharmaceutical pills, and marijuana.

2

Life in the 90's

Looking back to my high school years, I find it rather easy to pinpoint when and where my relationship to substances shifted for the worse. Life had been moving so quickly, and my social circles were constantly changing; not always for the better.

I thought my hometown was the center of the universe, and it was hard to imagine a world beyond Agawam, Massachusetts. As a young teenager, I spent my spare time skateboarding, jamming on instruments with friends and smoking pot. On the weekends, we either went to keggers in the woods or partied out by the lakes; all parts of the rural culture. My cousins who were about my same age lived nearby, only twenty minutes away and we were very close growing up.

My house was the hangout for the skaters. I had some grind rails and a mini-ramp in the backyard, and my friends always had a seat at the dinner table. Most of the weekdays were reserved for skating and getting back home at a reasonable hour, but the weekends were ideal for the teenager get-togethers. Around this time, you could see Staind and other bands play a show at a local hangout, Games and Lanes, for just a few bucks on a Friday night. Some of the other local punk bands would play gigs over in downtown Westfield at a couple of all age dive joints.

I had older brothers and sisters, long since moved out, and my parents weren't overly concerned about the pot smoking and beer drinking, so long as the neighbors weren't the ones telling them. My father was already in his 50's when I was born, and my mom, 22 years younger than him, had sustained a serious back injury years earlier. Most of the time she was laid up in pain, or coming and going from doctor's appointments. My sister Denise, from Mom's first marriage was ten years older than me, and she was living at home on and off through my teens.

For years my old man had been a mechanic for the local organized crime group; a small faction of the Genovese family based in New York. They operated out of downtown Springfield and he did financial collections and serviced backroom video poker machines, jukeboxes and pinballs all over Western Massachusetts, a job that he landed shortly after his first wife passed away back in the late 60's. His first children, three sons and two daughters, were significantly older than me. We were all a considerably close family, just a little spread out as far as age and geographical locations went.

My pops owned a bar for a short period in the late 1970's until a fire burnt the place down. He and his partner rebuilt, but the business never fully returned and he moved on from it shortly after meeting my mother, remaining employed with the Springfield crew.

He and my mother had met at another hangout up the road from his establishment in a roundabout way. After her shifts across the state line, my mom would stop off for a drink at the club where my grandmother worked. After some time she started to see my dad come around to service the barroom machines, and got the sense that maybe he would be interested in her mother, who had been widowed years earlier, and my mom tried to set them up. My old man fell for my mother instead, and despite the age difference, they went on to get married.

Over the years, I watched as my Dad came and went morning and afternoon to his work in the city. The outfit he worked for had a shop down on Main Street in the South End of Springfield that served as a legitimate front for the illegal video gambling activity that was the real backbone of the business, bringing in the money that was kicked up to the bosses. A lot of the machines that came and went from the location were pool tables, jukeboxes and other gaming equipment. Downtown Springfield isn't exactly well-known for its hospitality or low crime rate, and right around the corner from the shop on Main Street was the Saratoga neighborhood, a kind of one-way-in, one-way-out drug burdened project community.

My old man spent most of his time in and out of bars, collecting money out of the back room poker machines and servicing the front of the house amusement games. On days off from school or in the summertime, I'd go to work with my Dad, and that meant spending time in the company of low-level gangsters and frequenting bars and establishments all over the region. Most of the action was really in Springfield, and as a kid that resulted in my old man pumping quarters into an arcade game to keep me busy while he dealt with the more pressing matters of the poker machines. Kind of a dream come true for a 10-12 year old kid to sit in front of Street Fighter with unlimited credit play during the summer months, to say the least.

My dad was older at this point, in his mid-sixties, and a lot of people liked and trusted him. Some of the guys coined him with the nickname "Joey Pinball" and I fucking loved going into places with him. Even the somebody's and who's who of the organized crime scene had more trust in my old man than they did in their own affiliates. A lot of it had to do with my father needing some assistance in putting a down payment on the house before I was born, and some of the guys helped make that happen. After that, if they thought one of their own people had their hand in the cookie jar, they'd call my Dad to come in and run the numbers of cash in and payouts off the poker's internals, and it would point right back to some poor bastards shift, usually a nephew or shithead son-in-law skimming to buy a boat or trip to the horse track in New York. Only thing was, my dad was pretty well tied in and committed to being on call damn near 24/7 for those machines until he retired. Every other week he was on service calls, needing to be available to run to the city until late hours to resolve issues with poker machines to keep the money coming in for the crew.

To timestamp things, these were the years that MTV still did reasonable music programming. I would get up on a Saturday morning and wait for Rancid or one of the Seattle grunge bands like Nirvana or Alice in Chains to come on. After a while, my dad would get up and we'd head to Dunkin Donuts with an order for his boys down at Terry's Barber Shop in Westfield, then make the rounds to the bakeries to catch up with some of the Springfield players before lunch. Saturday afternoons were sometimes spent at these old Irish hangouts my pops liked, with the little twelve inch TVs behind the bar with reruns of The Three Stooges and old movies until the sports games came on. This was some kind of way for him to download with his people and let go of all the ridiculous stuff that went on with the crew on the other side of town. Sticky ass floors, smoldering ashtrays and jack-and-coke stained pool tables become a common weekend experience before I was a teenager.

Time spent with my Mom on the other hand, with her back pain and depression, didn't exactly prove as the most exciting of times in my life. We spent countless evenings after Dad's service calls in the ER for mom to get a shot of Demerol or cortisone to help with the pain.

I know now that my mother did everything she could within the limits of her pain and depression. Growing up we had great home-cooked New England boiled dinners, beef stew, and Italian dishes, even given her physical limitations, but any daylong activity she would get out of bed to do would put her back down for two more because of the pain. A childhood trip with Mom to the museum or Forest Park to feed the ducks during the day would usually end with my Mom laid up, and Dad and I throwing together one of his classic widower meals; usually some kind of meat and starch, and little to no vegetables.

Dinner with the old man was funny too. He'd say, "How about spaghetti and meatballs?"

"Sure dad." I'd say; and out came a can of Franco-American spaghetti and red sauce, no meatballs.

My mom and dad had a supportive, caring relationship, and looking back at it now, it had to be strange for my friends. My closest buddies that spent dinner at my place came from single family households and/or their parents worked late. My friends always liked spending time at my house and never seemed to tire of it; and it was cool for me because I didn't really like being alone. I got used to my sister Denise being at the house for a year or two and then she'd move out again; and frequenting my cousin's house on the weekend with two boys close in age made it rather difficult to come home to dad's work arrangement and mom's pain. Dad's work was enjoyable for me to an extent, but there was a lot he just didn't talk about. Not because he didn't want to, but because he couldn't. He had been through some serious shit losing his first wife followed by breaking his neck in a car wreck, and I think he was just happy and proud to be alive. He never really expressed much vulnerability, plus his work and the company that came with it didn't encourage emotional expression outside of the seemingly fixed, hardened mind states needed to get the job done and collecting money day in and day out.

I can recall some of the pre-teenage days I spent with my mother in the summers, and being this really creative kid doing puzzles and playing with Legos and such, but it sucked to not know if I was going to make it out of the house for an afternoon or to an activity with a friend. My mom really did take the time and effort to arrange stuff with the other neighborhood children's parents, but shit was just unreliable with her back pain. Emotionally she was challenging also. I really can't remember a time in a difficult emotional experience that I got asked by my mom, "How did that make you feel?" That stuff just wasn't talked about. How in the hell could you tactfully focus on anyone else when your suffering and discomfort is unbearable?

Both of my parents experienced loads of trauma; emotional, physical, sexual, you name it. Both of them had different instances where they just had to pick up the fucking pieces, carry on and provide. My dad lost both of his parents by age 22; my mother's dad was an alcoholic after Korea and died fairly young. Mom's first husband Richie was abusive; and Dad sure had his struggles trying to raise five kids after the loss of his wife Janet. Emotional unavailability is what I can see in my childhood looking back now. No blame here, just looking objectively at what was going on and how it all transpired. I'm glad I know how it affected everyone, and how it affected me, so I can continue to work with the truths of my childhood.

1992 was a rough year at home and around town. Lisa Ziegert, a local middle school teacher had gone missing shortly before Easter, and around the same time, my mom's younger brother Bobby, was hospitalized. The Lisa thing was crazy because some of the town kids had her as a teacher, and in a little place like Agawam and its 30,000 people, one person going missing is a big fucking deal. My Uncle Bobby on the other hand had a history of coming and going from regular family functioning, and it was pretty clear at my young age that he had personal difficulties. He was the baby of my mom's family, and probably handled all the childhood household shit the worst. The alcoholic dad, older siblings and growing up in the city likely contributed to a lot of his substance use. When he was around though he made sure to come see me and my cousins, Chris and Dean. I remember him walking with us up to the corner store for junk food just to spend some time with us. In my most vivid memories, he had a moustache and flowing brown hair down to about his shoulders, the tighter flannel shirts, pretty much straight out of the mid 80's, but he wore the shit out of that look and did it well.

I was at my sister's out by Tekoa Mountain in Westfield when my mom called to say she was coming to get me; Uncle Bobby had died. Within days, Lisa's body had been found in a turn off on the other side of town. It was all crazy at that age; Lisa's photos all over the news, and my last face to face with my uncle was him all jaundiced and bloated in a hospital bed. I remember being told at the time that he pretty much drank himself to death, but my mom finally came clean a couple years into my sobriety and said it was all due to heroin and crack.

Sadness and grief fell over my mom and her siblings for a while. It became apparent that her physical pain wasn't going anywhere anytime soon, and the death of her baby brother added all kinds of psychological pain. I recall a few surgical procedures over the years that provided temporary physical relief, but nothing would compare to the brief period like Mom's ability to function after taking a couple new to the market painkillers. This here is the beginning of my watching internal dilemmas being met with external solutions. Now this wasn't an epiphany at age twelve; this understanding came years later, understanding what I saw working with others when they needed to change the way they felt.

Around this time, Oxycontin was making it big as a so-called medical breakthrough, with doctors treating pain as the "fifth vital sign", the work of Purdue Pharma and the Sackler family.

My mom was getting 80 and 160mg Oxys prescribed to her the way one can buy aspirin; quite similar to buying bulk at Costco, and at a wholesale price. This started a whole era of shaping how substance engagement in my household and family would be viewed, accepted or stigmatized. Drugs, legal and illegal, inside and outside the home, were becoming more prevalent around my upbringing.

Shortly thereafter, the house that's backyard butted up against ours went up for sale, and when it sold, another kid a couple years older than me moved in with his mom and stepfather.

Mark's childhood had been pretty rough from my understanding, his biological father died young, his mom had a catering business and his stepdad owned a record store in Connecticut, but the parental relations and dynamic were interesting. His mom smoked pot, and so by the time Mark moved in at about age 14, he was heavy into weed himself. Mark would be one of the first guys that would introduce me to the older kids in school and those who dabbled with drugs and alcohol a little more than most. I think Mark's presence made my parents a little uneasy since you could see and smell the weed smoke from over the stockade fence; but he was also into BMX, skateboarding and we shared interests in music, so for the most part my parents kept their opinions to themselves. I started occasionally smoking weed with Mark and the older kids around our end of town.

For my mother, seemingly, with all the pain that she had endured, early along on Oxys it was like she was finally able to function a bit. My friends and I could get a lift to a warehouse skate park in Springfield, True East, from her a couple days a week. We had this little crew of skaters, Dan, Mickey, Jeff, Danny and me.

Every few days we'd meet up at my place, screw around on my equipment for an hour or so, and then head to the skate park. After work my old man would shoot over from downtown, scoop us up, and drop everybody back off at home. These were honestly some really fucking good times; they just were. We were all about our skating and the metal and punk music that was happening. None of us had girlfriends, we were all too caught up in where we were skating next and what tricks we had just learned to land. Some days, we'd jump on our BMX bikes, string our boards through our backpacks, and go set up shop at some busted up tennis court on the other side of Agawam. Then on Friday's a few of us would go with Mark and his stepdad to Whip City BMX, the bike racing track in Westfield for the Friday night races and hanging out.

In between all the skating, Mickey and I had this little band thing we were trying to get going. There was an older kid named Garrett that we started jamming with, trying to put together a metal group with his lyrics and our guitar playing. Garrett had some challenges going on at home and ended up crashing over at my place for a few months. He was that dress in all black, leather clad, bad looking dude that started to grow a beard at age 12. I'm not sure what yelled out to people that my place was a safe haven or that everyone was welcome, but it was just that. Garrett would be the first of three instances that somebody in some shit at their home came and stayed at mine.

Our practicing and search for a drummer went on for a bit, and during this time, I mustered up the courage to ask out a girl, Ariella, from class. "Asking out" at my age basically meant you were a couple, whether or not people actually did shit outside of school other than hold hands. Then again, what the hell do I know, I probably have it all wrong since I was a virgin until I was 19.

Garrett had been staying with my parents and me for a few months now, and along the way, Ariella and I ended up breaking up. Call me soft or whatever, but looking back now, I think I had a very difficult time getting attention and affection, then having it pulled away, as in the dynamic of "young love" or relationships so often unfolds. In all of this, Garrett had been around at times when Ariella was, and as in every other future case to come, it was those people closest to me that would snap the trust and brotherhood in half over their desire to have a relationship, and usually with the person I was interested in or dating.

This stuff all seems so trivial, even now. But to be truthful, it killed me, more and more every time it happened, another part of my hopes and ambitions fucking died with it.

Garrett had a part time gig at a gas station, and he left one particular afternoon to head off to work. I remember riding my bike to the other side of town to skate at my buddy Jon's one afternoon, and he lived on the same street as Ariella. At some point during the afternoon we had taken off in Jon's car to smoke some weed at a friend's, and as we passed Ariella's, I saw Garrett's red Ford in the driveway. He was walking out of the door of her blue raised ranch giving her kiss and heading to his car.

Just then, it felt like my stomach fell out onto the floor of Jon's sedan.

"Hey man, isn't that the Garrett dude that's staying with you?" Jon asked.

"Yeah man." I said.

I remember getting to the stop sign about three doors down and turning back, looking in absolute disbelief. How the hell could this guy go behind my back while living with me, and start to see my ex? Now this wasn't about her just being my ex, so much as it was that I didn't want to break up with her, and that Garrett was living in my fucking room at my parents' house with me.

Maybe it's just me as a critic of myself and thought process, or preconceived beliefs about human behavior that should deter someone as myself from thinking that this is a big goddamn deal. But it hurt so badly. Even though, some people said, "tough shit Joe, that's just life." Well, maybe it is, but that's not helpful, nor does it change the way I felt. The affection and warmth I felt for her and the other young women I would date would be the common emotions besides grief and loss that I would regularly get in touch with in my teenage years. I didn't possess any natural ability to act out in rage or revenge. My home was basically emotionless besides pain and the pursuit of relief; and at the end of the day, I believe each person in these pages, myself included, had just been trying to satiate some craving for pleasure, connection and intimacy.

I truly don't remember how the conversation unfolded between Garrett and me, but the whole thing with Ariella came up, and he moved out shortly after. Of course, the future of the band thing went right out the window with it, and I was fine with that. I think he finished out his junior year at Agawam High and moved on back to Connecticut sometime that summer.

Until now, it could have been viewed that I was a teenager "experimenting" with drugs and alcohol. I was smoking pot regularly with Mark and the guys. I had a job as a busboy at a local fine dining establishment that had some of the startup money kicked in by the Springfield crew, so I naturally became a shoe in and made good money for a fifteen year old bussing tables. When the local bosses or higher ups came in, they would request me to work their tables, fill their water, take plates, etc. and I would get slipped $5-$10 bills every time I leaned over to refill someone's glass. As soon as the tables were turned over for the evening, the waiters would announce their trip to the liquor store, and would offer to pick up something for me and my skating buddy, Dan, who was in the dish pit with my neighbor Mark. We would usually get some Captain Morgan and a bag of weed to take home and chill out with. On Sundays we'd get a lift out to the mall and blow our money hanging out and shopping for bullshit and stoner stuff at Spencer's.

During this time, one of the first considerably dangerous brush ups I had with drugs or alcohol was on an evening hanging out with Mark. We had been to a party out by the lakes and we cruised out there in Mark's little Dodge Neon with his pitbull. Somewhere in the evening a few of us had the bright idea to drive all the way to downtown Springfield on the rumor of a bar that was letting people in underage. Mark and I had to drop his dog off at his place before jumping on Route 57 to downtown, and we needed to get there with everyone else to make it through the door guy. We still had a half a rack of beer in the back seat; and both Mark and I were good and lit up already. He was hell bent on us getting out there quickly, and he started taking the turns out of the hill town into Agawam at about 60 mph, and he lost control by the revolver club that leads out towards the rock quarry. We spun out and that little Neon got rocketed through the woods a good fifty yards. When we finally stopped in the ditch; a four foot diameter oak tree had busted out my window and pushed the passenger side door and roof panel in a solid foot.

Being drunk already, I didn't immediately take in the gravity of our situation, outside of the fact we needed to get rid of the beer in the back seat, which had been spraying off like champagne since we hit the trees. Mark got out of his side with the dog fairly easily, and he tossed the opened beer cans further along and proceeded to unload the intact beer into one of the cars that had been following us and stopped to see if we were ok. As I climbed out of the driver's side and walked out to the road, I realized our headlights were glaring out of the ditch enough to bring concern to any other drivers.

I ran back down to the car and flipped off the lights, and Mark came back, finally wearing the shock of the whole thing, and said, "Hey, we gotta get the hell out of here, I think somebody else called in the accident, and they're gonna find the booze and then we'll be screwed."

We grabbed our things and started making our way through the woods with enough beer to make the trip worthwhile. Our hope was to get back to Mark's and sleep it off until we could figure out what to do about the car tomorrow.

We weren't at Mark's but ten minutes before his mom yelled downstairs, "Mark, where is your fucking car?"

"I left it at a friend's since I drank tonight mom."

"Are you sure it's not in a ditch out by the shooting range on the town line?" she asked.

Right then I decided to creep out the back door and hop the fence back to my place. I'd had enough for one night.

Outside of that incident, life outside of home at this time was pretty consistent. School, skate, work, music, kick back, and a little pot and booze trickled in. I had a ton of friends, in every social circle that existed in school; older, younger, skaters, jocks, preps, you name it and I was cool with them all. I've always been truly fortunate to forge relationships with different groups of people, no matter what their background or interests. There are very few occasions where I couldn't connect to people. My problem was staying connected to myself, to my goals and aspirations, and being patient and understanding of myself and the things that I experienced. I just feel like in trying to build all those relationships I was really trying to figure out who I was. Though I had all of those friends, I never really felt like an actual member of any of those groups. On the surface it may have looked as if I was, but I always felt like I was on the fringe and experienced insecurity around that. And in all of it, I lost sight of who and what I wanted to be in light of who I thought I wasn't.

The remaining years of high school are a cumulative mix of substance and relationship experimentation that would eventually lead to isolation from people and a sense of "ok-ness" when I drank or used.

3

The Beginning 1999-2001

Some of this is bizarre to reflect and write about; trying to re-visit how these friendships started, and where they went after certain events. My drug use and stuffing of emotions has long since totally capsized the initial happier phases of these relations. For the first couple years of my recovery, I was really only able to re-call the bitter end of the relations. I want to be clear now that many of the characters and I have reconciled, largely in part to the amends process and my growth in understanding of our human condition. Surely looking back in the moment, I felt like a victim. How could this shit not feel personal? It absolutely had to be, or else people just wouldn't behave this way.

Reality check: life is impersonal. How I have responded to life made it personal. Believe it or not, that's great news for an addict like me. That means many of my problems are of my own making. If they're of my making, that means I can do something about them. If they're of someone else's making, I'm stuck wait-ing around for others to fix shit in my life. Thankfully though, the latter is not the case.

As for things in my household, my mom's OxyContin use was through the roof. She had been steadily prescribed the narcotic for some time now, and the nodding off in conjunction with her sleep apnea left her like a zombie most of the time. I would often come home on the weekends to her falling over, having nodded off or fallen asleep standing up. Once she even came to after having fallen head first onto our raised edge fireplace. There were cigarette burns scattered in the kitchen linoleum and I felt like I didn't know my mother much through these times. I remember some of the nights that my dad came out of his bedroom just trying to get my mom to put the cigarettes out and lay down on the couch. It finally got to the point she started smoking over the kitchen sink with the window open, a half-assed security measure so the ash wouldn't land on something that would catch fire easily. For a couple of years there seemingly every time I came home late in the evening, my first contact through the door was with my mother doped up and nodding off.

Things finally got so bad that she began asking me if I knew where to get any Oxys in between her scripts. I'm not mad at my mother for it; I never was. I just realize that this isn't the kind of stuff that happens in healthy households. None of my close friend's parents that I knew were asking them where to score drugs. But in the interests of wanting to relieve my mother's pain that I didn't understand spanned beyond the physical, I willingly took up the task. Eventually after it came out to my dad that I had gone and gotten her some, he took it upon himself to go to the guys in the Springfield crew about other ways to acquire the pills in between scripts.

Here's what stands out to me now: we didn't talk about what was wrong with this picture, what this meant to send a sixteen year old on an errand to illegally buy prescription narcotics. The main thing was that we discussed how to try to get my mother some relief from her pain, that there was a more cost friendly way through my dad's associates. That's what life around my home was always like, how to be in less pain, and in this case at a lesser cost. It felt as though we were always looking for the next surgery, pill or pain management method for my mother. And by now though at the turn of the century, most pain management recommended by doctors was an opiate.

I never referred to my mom as an addict during that time because she just wasn't viewed as such, with prescription in hand. Good doctors were simply expected to help provide relief for their patients. It's amazing what we know now about the beginning of the overprescribing wave and what crisis would follow; that it wasn't largely anticipated that white American families were about to become the common faces of addiction for years to come in America. After the traumas and incarceration Blacks endured with crack in the 80's, to see this epidemic unfold, that it would be met with compassion and a desire to help, solely based on whites now being affected, I can't even imagine what it could have been like to grow up with the stigma and criminalization that came with being Black and addicted, or being the teens or children in those households in the '80s and '90s. White privilege is alive and well in the way we view addiction and who is worthy of treatment. At least in how I was brought up at home, in a town comprised of being 93% white, the way my dad spoke about things like addiction and crime, he had a regular tendency to refer to those as issues or problems that happened over in Springfield and were associated with the Puerto Rican and Black communities, on that side of the Connecticut River.

Do you think we were ever taught the truth about the experiences of Black, brown and Indigenous communities, and the horrors of colonization in my high school? Fuck no. I remember our social studies books and their brief sections on slavery and the Civil Rights Movement, as if they were strictly elements of the past and everything was just better for everyone since. There was very little encouragement to recognize and learn about other cultures and communities, like the local indigenous populations, let alone how whitewashed our history lessons were. As I reflect back on living and growing up there I can see the blame and apathy was so pronounced; and it still is. To empathize and consider the causes and conditions of other's difficulties that weren't white like us would unseat suburban life as we knew and had lived it.

It wasn't just the local news outlets and my dad that were peddling blame on Black and brown folx; this was a common experience to hear about in the company of other local kids and their parents. There was an unspoken fear and frustration about the city over the river in our suburban households. I had been explicitly taught to trust and believe that those communities were the root of the world's problems; and subconsciously addiction would become a word for a condition that was just not experienced by white people, or at least not by our white middle class town. Sure, we had alcoholism in my family, but addiction just wasn't going to make its way into the vocabulary of our household as something we were dealing with; not for some time.

Nothing could have been further from the truth of the matter. Imagine if my mother had been a person of a darker skin color, prescribed Dilaudid and then finding out she was pregnant with me; what would the doctor's and community response and perception of us had been? There would have been child welfare services all over us.

White American, middle class, and privileged; and that identity experience was about to detrimentally contribute to the on-going disbelief many American's felt when their seemingly good suburban or rural kids became strung out in the early 2000's, resting in the good faith of their family physicians and the contents of their home medicine cabinet. As young people would wander their way from the medicine chest to the more populated cities looking for cheaper narcotics and addiction took hold, the blame got worse. Many American families didn't have the ability to look at their role in writing off their loved one's behavior and looked for a person or group to scapegoat. White supremacy as it relates to behavioral health and the war on drugs has been taught and learned in American households, especially in rural communities, and has led many families to hold the expectation that they would be shielded and unaffected by drug addiction; that we were above it.

In the escalation of my mother's pill consumption I met Jenn through my skating bud Dave, both of them a year behind me as a sophomore, and we started hanging out on Fridays. One of her parents would bring her by with her friend Ashley, and we would all kick it for a few hours over a couple beers or smoking bowls in the woods behind my house. During this time, my interest and affection for Jenn grew rapidly.

That spring, my cousin Chris introduced me to his baseball teammate, Andy. Andy, Jenn, Ashley and I all started spending time together that summer while Chris went off to sports camps. Andy had a little red Honda with a cd player, and we used to roll around up in the hills going to swimming holes and smoking weed.

Before long, unbeknownst to me, Jenn and Andy were catching feelings for each other, and I got ditched a random Friday night. Neither of them had answered their phones, so I called my friend Al and he came and scooped me up for a bit. Right after we left my parents place, we pulled into the Dairy Mart convenience store up the road, and there were Andy and Jenn sitting in the red Honda.

I immediately felt like shit. I glanced over to the car, totally forgetting what we had even stopped at the store for, turned my head back, and Al and I pulled off. It wasn't too difficult to disconnect from them for a while at that point. I just felt disowned and unwanted.

Eventually Jenn came around again, and she was apologetic so we jumped back into hanging out. This went on for a couple of months before I had the nerve to ask her out at the local fair event, The Big E, and she said yes. Within two weeks, we were at a house party in my neighborhood at her friend's place down the street, and there was this awkward tension in the air between us that I couldn't figure out. I thought maybe it was the underage sense that Agawam PD could be showing up at any second to break up the party, but not much more.

Finally she let me know that she still had her interests in Andy and she couldn't stay on with me. I think I took it the best I could, and we continued on as good friends anyways.

But just shortly after, only a month or two later, she and Chris got friendly and began dating.

One evening he called me up to say, "Hey man, I know you really have a thing for Jenn, and you two have a little past, but she and I are really into each other. I thought I should call to check in with you about it, out of respect."

To be honest, it was pretty upsetting for a while, but what the hell, they were happy. My problem was that I didn't know how to process emotions in a positive way, and I held onto my grief and frustration with no healthy outlet. Most of the people around me chimed in to tell me that I should just be happy for them; but I didn't know how.

There was another solid blow or two to come though. I met Nicole when I was Junior; and she was really who I remember as my high school sweetheart. The whole thing actually lasted a while; it had prom in there, and our parents got to know each other a bit, that kind of thing.

She was a freshman, and her parents were divorced. Her dad was this Dwayne Johnson looking guy with a classic Pontiac convertible, and her mother was a beautiful 40 year old version of her. Nicole had long brown hair, tan skin, super skinny figure and the best laugh. We had what felt like a picture perfect high school relationship: being a couple at our lockers in between classes, going to parties on the weekends, and cruising around in my '93 Honda Accord with the sunroof open cranking music at night; singing along together and admiring one another. Also at this point my parent's permitted little gatherings in our base-ment; drinking, smoking and playing pool, and a bunch of us we're getting together as couples, including Chris and Jenn, and a few others.

That winter of '99-00 had been a harsh one. On Super Bowl Sunday my sister Denise had been in a bad car accident, mixed up with the road conditions and she and her boyfriend John dri-ving under the influence, and she wound up living back at home recovering from the injuries for some months. During this time she was doing a lot of blow and drinking almost every night, and I could hear the sniffs and vodka and soda being poured over ice in corner store cups from the room next to mine. I was living in a household fully engulfed in substance use disorders in search of relief.

I felt really awful for my sister, knowing that just a couple of years earlier her ex took custody of the kids. My family had spent the better part of the kid's younger years helping her support and raise them while her ex had been out drinking, getting DUI's and doing whatever the hell he wanted between jail and working out of state. He hadn't showed up much as a parent and Denise had been working waiting tables and trying to finish school to make a life for her and the kids. She had a reality that was just plain diffi-cult and I think anybody would have sought some kind of escape from the way things unfolded for her.

Around the end of summer in 2000, the head of the company my Dad worked for, (and boss of other things on the local level) along with a few associates, were indicted on federal charges in association with the poker machines and organized crime.

I had come home after a long night out, and just went into my room to crash when my mom came rushing in.

"Get up, it's serious! They just arrested Albert and the feds are at the shop in Springfield!" she said.

"Where's Dad?" I asked.

"He's with Don, they are out collecting the money. I just spoke with him. They know the arrests are happening and the police are only a couple steps behind them. The feds and cops are raiding the bars and clubs with the poker machines, taking the equipment and looking for the money as evidence."

The rest of that day was kind of a blur. Dad had some footprint in our work shed that he had been building some of the machines from scratch at home to put out on location, so I had to hide the parts and stash the bill acceptors and electronic circuit boards.

Dad and Don managed to stay ahead of the authorities for a couple days. As for the business itself, it was never quite the same after the indictments that followed.

Things got really hairy around the household for a while, and money was really tight as everybody close to the operation had been watched, including my Dad. The leadership within that circle was also starting to take a shift, with violence and murder directed at taking out some of the local higher ranking individuals. A lot of the future of my Dad's income, safety and security was compromised both at work and in his personal health.

My Dad had been diagnosed with cancer in the midst of all this, and it surely stirred up a lot of worry in the family. Two of his siblings had already lost their battle with cancer in previous years. The stress mounted within the household from financial difficulties around Dad's work, his cancer treatment and the ups and downs of OxyContin controlling my mom's life. Having my sister there helped us feel like somehow we were all doing our best to help one another, and that's probably true to some extent. For me though, I was getting accustomed to substances and the behaviors around them in my household. Everybody was on some sort of "treatment" for one thing or another.

Early in my senior year, my friend Jay had started staying at my place. He had gotten the boot from his parent's for smoking pot, and his mom and step dad weren't about to have that with his younger brother growing up in the house. Denise and John had been able to move on, and Dad had stabilized a bit with the cancer treatments, so I guess we were just getting used to having folx that needed help always moving in with us.

Jay and I had hung out a lot over the last two years on and off. He and I split my room, worked together for a bit at the local transmission parts shop after school, but our circle of close friends differed enough that we had some space between us. He had been at my place so long that my mom even had him in on the household chores. My parents really had a soft spot for wanting to see him finish out high school, and it was pretty cool to have him around.

Nicole and I went to prom in 2001, and it's funny the way things ended up and who was all there. Ariella went with my buddy Billy, our neighborhood car mechanic, and Chris and Jenn went too. Pretty funny turn of events, but also goes to show how quickly we tend to resolve shit on the superficial level in high school. We had about two or three other couples in the limo, and the driver hired by my dad was this funny little Danny

DeVito type character, Artie. Some kind of four foot nine friend of the Springfield crew with a limo business.

Things were rolling steady with Nicole all the way up towards my graduation. I even remember having the talk with her father about my proposed direction after high school, for concern of who and what his daughter was getting involved with. It began to feel like things were coming together.

The night before my graduation party my old man wanted to go out and catch a movie with me, and Nicole went to hang out at a friend's house.

I got up that Saturday morning, after barely sleeping with the excitement of the celebration to come. My dad was going to pick up the keg with Denise and John, who had become like a big brother the last three years. John was about thirteen years older than me and was known for having big house parties over in West Springfield. I even sold pot for him for a short period of time when they first met.

Robbie and Renee showed up, super close friends of mine that lived close to Billy the mechanic. Robbie and I rolled over to pick up Nicole at her mom's. When we got there, Nicole was out back where she would sometimes smoke cigarrettes.

As I walked up, I noticed she looked really distraught, and as I went to embrace her she was a little distant.

"Are you ok, is everything alright?" I asked, as she started shaking her head.

I began to wonder if something happened with a family member.

She sat there crying for about ten minutes, with all kinds of crazy ideas going through my head of what could have possibly been wrong.

Finally she said, "Joe, I have to tell you something." and I froze up.

"I cheated on you last night." she sobbed.

"Are you fucking kidding me? With who Nicole?"

She wouldn't tell me, and a good fifteen minutes went by where I was absolutely ferocious inside and I walked away, back to my car to cool off. Robbie went and spoke with her and somehow that helped her get up the courage to tell me.

"DJ." she said.

I couldn't believe it. I had just hung out with DJ the week before, he knew we were together, and his cousin was coming to my grad party in the next few hours.

I don't really remember much else from that morning, other than telling her that she still needed to come and my family was expecting her.

There was a lot of alcohol and good company. Most of the day was a pretty good time, as friends and family came and went. There were other grad parties that weekend so a lot of people were making the rounds in groups, stopping off and moving along to the next party.

But the one thing I really noticed looking back was that after all was said and done, after everybody else left and had crashed out, the one thing that didn't fail to leave my side was alcohol. My last clear memory of that big day was sitting up all night in my backyard, eventually drinking alone until three or four in the morning. As frustrated as I was with Nicole earlier the day before, after all the turmoil of having to share that news and have the trust broken on one of the most important days of my life so far, alcohol did for me what I couldn't do for myself. It gave me some relief, took the edge off, and made it so I could care less that my whole world was being turned upside down. Until now I had only drank because it was a thing to do; not because I felt like I needed it to survive.

Jay hadn't been at my grad party for long; and our hopes were that his parents would let him come back home after seeing him finish school, but he moved out about three days after the party to start staying with a friend over in West Springfield.

Nicole and I hadn't spoken much since she left in the evening of the grad party. I was kind of going through the motions of figuring out what was next, trying to enroll myself at community college in Springfield, even though I had barely made it out of high school. My grades weren't the best, and I had recently put a lot of energy and effort into the other relationships in my life, Nicole and Jay, amidst the chaos in my household. Trying to finish school and move along in life with Nicole as my girlfriend and helping Jay towards graduation, my gears started to shift away from doing what I needed to do to be setting myself up for life after high school. Things with my dad's career and work had pretty much come to a halt, and I couldn't see myself wasting any of his money on a half attempt at education that I had no idea what I would do with, even if I could hold my academics together for another two to four years.

I don't recall exactly who I heard it through, but about a week after Jay moved out, there was a party at Nicole's house. Her mom was out of town on a trip, and she and Jay ended up sleeping together. Word traveled fast back to me about that one.

I was fucking broken. I was at a place where I just didn't understand people, especially the people in my life; the ones I loved, the ones I helped, the ones I trusted.

Again, I get it. It's life, right? Tough shit, move on, plenty of fish etc. I didn't give a damn, I didn't want other women, I didn't want other friends, I just wanted the ones in my life to have some integrity, respect and to not betray me.

This was all too much. We graduate high school and the world suddenly casts expectations on us. I remember my older family members asking me at the party, "What are you going to do with yourself now Joe? Done with high school and all, what's next? What college are you going to?"

I should have responded with, "Well now that you mention it, my first real intimate relationship has gone to hell, so I think I'll continue to drink so I don't have to feel that shit; and while I'm at it, I plan to develop an inseparable bond with cocaine so I can leave this life behind and meet some new friends that deal the stuff because the shit makes me feel nice, and I'd like some more of it."

Because that's what happened next.

Prior to these events, I drank, I smoked pot, and a good share of it; similar to a lot of other kids in my town. At parties on the weekends, maybe even an occasional beer or two if somebody had some stashed on a school night. I even tried cocaine a good ten times before my life got derailed and these substances provided exactly what kind of relief I needed. I truly believe that I was not "hardwired for addiction" or "had the genes". I think there's a piece of it that can be related to that, but I don't see it as the primer for my addiction. For me, it came down to what Gabor Mate says: it was my best attempt to solve a problem in my life, and my relational change to drugs and alcohol happened overnight, literally. This regularly happens to adults, whose life or relationships fall apart later on down the road, into their 30's or 40's; so why minimize the pain of these experiences just because one is young?

Right there at the grad party, and the morning after, when that alcohol was still there by my side. Everything I had watched with my mother reaching for those external solutions for internal dilemmas. This is how addiction came to fruition in my life.

Shortly after the graduation party, my parents went on a two week trip to Portugal. My sister and John were slated to help take care of the house along with me until my parents returned. For the next two weeks, they had their coke dealers over daily and we drank, snorted, and partied day and night. I blew the $1300 in money I had received in grad gifts on alcohol and blow like it was fixing my fucking life, because, well, at that time, it was. By the time my parents returned, I didn't have a dime left of that money.

To be honest, I was scared, but not of the drugs and alcohol. Anytime I was sober I had to deal with the fact the people that had just been closest to me had totally screwed me over, emotionally. And now, life is asking "what are you going to do with yourself?" Life doesn't wait for the wounds to heal, it doesn't ask if the timing could be better. Everything was suddenly overwhelming and I felt fucking lost. How am I supposed to live up to whatever it is I'm supposed to do? It seemed like a damned miracle that I was the last kid of seven and I managed to graduate high school. Just two years earlier I wanted to drop out, then I met Nicole, then Jay moved in. And now both of those relationships went to hell, simultaneously.

Now, I had found a way to take flight from the recent painful realities I didn't want to deal with, and I could, so long as I had the means. I was only interested in who was buying my alcohol and where and when I was meeting the coke connect. I wouldn't allow myself to process the resentments I buried until 14 years later.

4

Delivery of Heroin

I'm not sure if I'd consider my experience of being arrested that morning traumatic outside of being handcuffed, as it's surely unpleasant to not have willful use of your hands. Of course this instance could have felt differently had guns been drawn, but that was not part of this morning's events. The task force swooped in and before I knew it I had been cuffed and put into squad car, as the large SUV with the jump out team headed up the road.

When we got downstairs at the station, I was brought into a room that was crawling with feds and local police. They had a large board that had pictures of suspects and numbers below them. It looked like something out of The Sopranos or The Wire, when the cops are trying to build a case against a criminal organization. For a brief moment I felt like a celebrity. The officers tried to straighten my bandana, and then they handed me a small piece of paper with a number on it, and below the number it said "arrested" and the date. They told me to hold it up to my chest while they snapped a photo of me, and they went on to place some of my info up on the big board.

I remember standing there in awe, like I had made the big leagues or some shit. There had to be well over a hundred individuals on there, lots of familiar faces from the block. I remember looking over at the brown paper bag of evidence they took off me, and realized they were testing the little bit of crack I had. By the time they had gotten to me, I wasn't exactly a successful dealer, holding a bunch of "walking around dope" for my smoking pleasure. I was such a burnt out, foul smelling junkie that if I was holding $1.50 and there was a push left on the pipe, I was well aware of both.

They took me to a holding cell with a handful of other guys, and next to us were another two or three cells. Nobody spoke a word to each other. I remember being so uncomfortable because I was already feeling dope-sick that morning, and now I had my hands wrenched behind my back. I sat down on the floor and proceeded to try and get my cuffed hands out to the front of me by crunching my knees in as far as I could. I was successful, and for about five minutes I was able to ease the discomfort in my wrists and shoulders.

"Hey man what the hell do you think you're doing? Stand up, and turn around, you've gotta keep your hands behind your back."

The cell door opened, and a plain-clothes officer came in and cuffed me again in the back.

He looked at me and said, "You ever heard of LEAD? Somebody from LEAD is going to come talk to you in a few minutes."

I looked up and said, "I'm not ratting on anybody so don't waste your time."

He just shrugged and walked off. For a second there I fancied myself having some kind of street integrity and pride, like I knew something and had some honor to show off.

LEAD (then known as Law Enforcement Assisted Diversion) is a local program that was kicked off a few years earlier, meant to help out small repeat drug offenders, committing crimes of survival i.e. prostitution, low level drug dealing etc. utilizing a harm reduction model, meeting individuals where they're at. There was this narrative on the street that some of the LEAD participants were confidential informants. How the hell else could someone commit so many drug related offenses and stay out of custody? "Tell on three, go free" was what people used to say about LEAD out on the Blade.

Anyways, the person from LEAD never showed up to talk to me, and the next time the cell door opened, a handful of us were shipped over to King County Correctional Facility. The first court hearings were said to be over a week away.

Over the next ten days, I would be housed with roughly twenty people I knew from the downtown streets. Dizzy was the first one I saw when I got to the Ninth floor South wing at county correctional. We were both brought upstairs at the same time, and picked close bunks to talk about the sweep and our cases.

The downtown Seattle correctional facility is a terrible place, in my opinion, and not just because it's a jail. Not really that I'm proud to have preferences in where I get locked up, but I do. My experience is only at the county level; but I'd have to say that the Maleng Regional Justice Center in Kent, WA is where I'd rather end up. The Seattle jail is smack-dab in the middle of downtown, and you can end up with views of Elliot Bay or I-5, where you can watch people walk up the hill into the homeless encampments and score dope; essentially getting well while you are typically in withdrawal behind bars. Most of the time in the processing phase or short stays, you end up in a pod with about 20-30 other guys, no commissary or store. Yard out is only once or twice a week, with no overhead sunlight and you'd be lucky to get a haircut, yard or commissary unless you were there over two weeks. Plus it's cold as hell in the winter.

Dizzy and I talked about who else we saw get bagged on the block, and what the potential outcomes at court could be, those kinds of things. Most of the first two days were interrupted sleep, cold sweats and dry heaving. After a solid couple months of running and gunning without getting picked up, it's easy for the body to call it quits and sleep for a solid 24 hours but then the withdrawal would really set in for me. Every single night that first couple of weeks (when I would actually be able to get some rest) was spent dreaming about heroin. Vivid dreams too, the kind in which I was getting released, walking out the door and the dealer is waiting for me dope dreams. Scoring, just about to get right, and then, poof, I'd wake up; still dopesick.

In the county jail, there are a lot of "jailhouse lawyers" too. A whole bunch of illegal behavior with a shit ton of courtroom experiences, telling you how your next hearing is gonna go down. "Oh yeah, you won't serve on that", or, "You'll do three months, and with good time be out in a month and half", or "they'll offer you drug court; don't do it, it's a set-up." I heard that one a lot, especially with the size of the recent bust. Lots of talk of drug court. How difficult it was, how long and impossible the program can be, how hard the prosecutor is if you don't complete it. Basically I didn't hear anything that was encouraging a path out, other than eating the felony charges and doing some time down in Shelton or wherever one got placed for anything over a 365 day sentence. Best case scenario after that was I could get out and connect with the guys I spent these last two weeks hearing it all from, and they'd put me on with a new dope hook up. Needless to say, I was not surrounded by sound solutions to my increasingly problematic situation.

Finally, the day came when a bunch of us were arraigned. The morning started off as usual; breakfast, announcement of the day's court hearings, clean up routine, some bullshitting within the pod, sleep for a bit, then lunch. Three or four of us were finally called out into the central area by the guard station. The ninth and tenth floors are set up so that there are about four pods per floor, and in the middle of all of the pods like a central hub, sat a raised guard station. When it came time for hearings, all the inmates waiting for court would be pulled off to one side of the guard station by a hallway that led to the elevators. You might have two guards for ten or twelve guys, and they would take us up to the top floor to catch the sky bridge that acts as a safe throughway from the jail to the courthouse, two blocks to the west. No windows, just a long narrow corridor that serves as easily monitored transport without the need for vehicles and exit or reentry to the jail or courthouse.

We were all pulled into a bullpen, or waiting room for our court appearance. As we were waiting, three or four more pods of guys from the bust were hauled into the bullpen. It was like a Third Ave reunion; quick handshakes, warm hellos and cold stares circled the room as more of the outlying benches became crammed with bodies. A couple of attorneys made their way into the staging area with another two officers and they started calling out names. They had a stack of discoveries and police reports. Suddenly the room fell quiet, as the paperwork got handed out. It was like the last day of grade school in June and report cards just got handed out, and some kids were finding out what degree of ass whooping and summer grounding was going to be put on them when they turned the grades over to their parents.

One of the familiar faces, this kid Joey about 18 years old, came over to me with his paperwork, and said, "Hey man, I think they got us in the same case."

We started comparing the officer names, times/dates and sure enough Joey had gotten "Solicitation to commit VUCSA", or in layman's terms, telling or showing someone where they could buy dope. As for me, mine read "VUCSA delivery". Violation of the Uniform Controlled Substances Act, delivery or sale of heroin to an undercover officer/confidential informant.

Joey and I walked our way through our history out on the street, which spanned a few months. He was this scrawny dark haired kid with a young mother who herself had spent some years strung out. For an eighteen year old, he had pretty good street credit. A lot of people vouched for him and he was quick to help get you well if he knew you. Occasionally he would bring me sales or introduce me to someone who was trying to push dope to the street dealers who could move it quickly, which for a while I was. We even kinda laughed about it as we recalled the day's events that the case was built on. Looking around the room, some guys were hashing out details and starting to get frustrated;

blaming and the occasional "snitch ass-motherfucker" were heard as people somehow assumed their counterpart was at fault for bringing a confidential informant or undercover to buy dope off of them. It didn't serve Joey or I to be pissed at each other, hell, we were both in the same boat up shit's creek, except his charge carried a lighter sentence.

Courtroom for arraignment we were heading into: Drug Diversion Court.

5

Navy Recruit

The remainder of that summer of 2001 was really one of the most life-changing periods of my life so far due to personal circumstances and world events.

A couple times shortly after the honeymoon weeks with cocaine I had tried to get together with Nicole, just to catch up and see how things felt, and I could never get past the hurt I felt from the betrayal. Not just from that relationship, but everything that happened those final years of high school. I was already getting accustomed to my life with drugs in it, and I wasn't making much space for friends and family anymore. There was one positive person that entered my life at this time though.

Amy and I had a class together my junior year. She was a senior, and the younger sister of my friend Erik. Long blonde hair, blue eyes, and she was incredibly fun to hang out with. She had come to my grad party, and given that was a messy time and all, I managed to stay in touch with her over the first few weeks following. She also worked with my sister Denise for a bit at a local Friendly's restaurant so there was some sense of security with her, like she was safe to be around for me, knowing my sister and being Erik's family. We went to the beach, hung out 'til the early hours of the morning, kicked it over at my sister and John's, and ended up getting really close over the course of a couple months. Some nights we would take drives out on the back roads of Connecticut listening to music, often for hours at a time.

There's something warming about spending time with someone and knowing without words having to be said between you both, that you just vibrate on the same frequency. I'm not sure what the frequency was, but maybe it was just a desire we both had to be our genuine selves, and we could be that in each other's presence.

Eventually though, my ongoing commitment to cocaine and alcohol really had a hold of my life, and as much as I had fallen for her, I really didn't have what it took to be in a relationship. If I could have allowed her into my life as much as she was willing at that time, maybe things would have been different. The part that really hurt the most is Amy was the one person that would continue to encourage me to do right by myself for myself, not for anyone else. It's really upsetting to not actually know how to do that, but really wishing you could. She's always been there, and has never given up on trying to pull me out of my gutters.

By the end of August, I had made the decision not to go to community college. I had absolutely no clue what I was interested in besides getting high, and I wasn't about to spend whatever little money my parents had getting poor grades, if I was to attend classes at all.

Amy's brother got me hired on at a grocery warehouse down in Windsor Locks by the airport, and I started making pretty decent money for a short period of time. I was doing incentive-based order selecting with a team of four or five other guys, and I started spending a lot of time with one of them.

Marty was a serious night owl, and he just moved back from Florida working in nightclubs and was really into ecstasy and coke. We worked nights at the time and we spent our evenings off doing E and hanging out with other guys he knew that used and sold it.

In early fall I began working day shift and took my lunch break to run up the road and grab some pizza. When I came back to the office to grab my order sheet, I asked my supervisor a question and he turned around real quick and he said, "Wait, wait shut up for a second."

Then I realized everyone was fixated on the TV, dead silent. It was roughly 10:30 a.m. on September 11th, and the North Tower of the World Trade Center had just collapsed. My mother was actually working minimal hours as a parking booth attendant at the airport around this time, and Bradley International Airport immediately shut down operations for the day. Most of us at C&S Wholesale just went on to finish the first shift in an awkward state of shock and wondering if some plane that left the airport down the road was part of this whole mess.

After 9/11, I started kicking around the idea of joining the military. My father was encouraging me, saying "you ought to join before Bush drafts your ass over there and you don't get to pick what branch you go to." Plus I had a couple cousins who had joined the service, and so far they had pretty good things to say about the travels and structure.

I was spending my weekends over by the lake with Marty from C&S and had gotten hooked up with some other coke-heads. Marty was on a solid night crew team and the day shift team I had gotten placed on wasn't working out, and I stopped making a good paycheck. I figured I ought to find something else until I can make a decision about this military thing.

One of the girls I knew through Marty referred me for a gig as a lot boy/detail guy at a car dealership in Westfield that she worked the service desk at. The highlight was that my new coworker Jose had a connection that would bring blow by the lot anytime we wanted, and would trade us for the cd players that came in on trade-in vehicles. Basically a lot of the dope was free.

Jose and his brother were knowledgeable auto maintenance guys. Things like brakes, belts and other odds and ends were easy jobs for them, and they would land side gigs on the weekend. A lot of times they would need a lift over to pick up a vehicle, run for parts and drop the vehicle back off to the owner, so I would make myself available.

Jose was also heavy into heroin, so maintaining his habit required cash 24/7. One Saturday afternoon, we had to drop a Honda Civic to its owner in Holyoke. I don't know how much it's changed, if at all, but Holyoke was like the heroin capitol of western Mass in 2001. Jose regularly scored his dope up in this area, but it was a hell of a bus ride for him, and I would get paid in coke for my help with the rides and car work so this was a good deal for both of us.

"Hey, I'm just gonna roll up and drop off the keys, and he's got something for both of us, so we don't need to go anywhere else after this, cool? You just need to hang tight and keep your head down around here, got it?" Jose said.

"Yeah sounds good." I said.

"K I'll be right back."

"Gotcha." I replied.

Jose walked up about half a block, went into a five or six floor apartment building, and I just sat there flipping through my cd's for a good ten minutes like I was reading a book. Jose was about 42 when I first met him, and given the nature of how long he had been in the drug game, I did my best to listen when he gave me directives, especially when it came to being in certain neighborhoods where he was used to scoring. I remember my palms being a bit sweaty and just feeling uneasy about the whole thing. Kind of this, "Don't do this and don't do that, but I'll be right back."

What the fuck am I supposed to do with that, if something goes down?

After a good 10-12 minutes, I heard some commotion coming from one of the windows. The building had one of those switchback stair-wells that went up the center of the building with windows open over the platforms in between the flights of steps. It sounded like two guys arguing, but it was difficult to make out what was being said.

Finally a half a minute or so later the door to the building flew open and all I remember seeing was the back of a dark colored jacket and a hand going up in the air.

"Pop, pop...pop, pop, pop."

Holy shit. I knew right away what I heard. I couldn't help picking my head up and looking towards the door. Was it Jose and another guy, or just somebody else all-together?

I remember seeing the guy's foot still holding the door as he lay on his back, motionless. He was across the sidewalk entrance to the building but the main door couldn't close. I watched as another guy stepped out over the body, put a pistol into his waistband, and took off up the block.

Within seconds, Jose poked his head through the door, looked both ways, stepped over the body and walked towards the car as I hit the unlock button.

Jose got it in and said, "Man, that's why you don't rip people off in this game. Let's get the fuck outta here."

As I started to pull away from the curb and get onto 391, the sun was setting. I watched a guy get got shot in broad daylight on a Saturday afternoon. No sirens, no commotion on the street. Just the cost of doing bad business with the wrong person. It was like buying a pack of gum for Jose, like it hadn't been his first time witnessing a murder.

"Those guys were arguing in the stairwell when I went up to Andre's. Something about one guy selling the other guy some bad shit. Look how that ended." Jose said as he reached into his pocket and handed me a little blue bag with a chunk of coke in it. He tucked his head down by the glove box, stuck a four inch straw into his little grey envelope and took a blast of his stuff, and nodded on off for a good twenty minutes.

I drove the fifteen minutes back to West Springfield, replaying that whole scene that took place that afternoon, only to drive back up there four hours later for more drugs for the both of us, like none of it ever happened.

I worked the car dealership job through the winter, with my dad riding my ass most of it about my lack of direction. I met another young woman early into that work, and she was in the circle with the crew I was running around with on the weekends. We would go out drinking out in the hill towns at outdoor or house parties every weekend, like clockwork. Thing for me was after about three drinks I developed an irresistible desire for blow, and the problem was, she hated coke. Within two to three months she'd had enough of looking for me at a get-together only to find me in somebody's car with my head face down on a cd case full of white powder with a rolled up dollar bill.

By March I had enlisted in the US Navy. My Dad had been a sailor back in Korea, so I figured as far as making him happy, joining the same branch ought to get him off my back and make him proud all at the same time.

There was a big sense of patriotism after 9/11 and it was real easy to get a nineteen year old wound up to go and "kick some foreign ass". Man was I naive; but hey, they reeled me in good. I got tied up with the same recruiter that put my two cousins in, and I was signed and ready to go in two weeks.

Leading up to that date of departure to boot camp, I felt like I was trying to do enough drinking and drugging to cover my need to not do any for the next four years that I was about to sign away.

The night before I was slated to get picked up to go to the Military Entry Processing Station (MEPS) I had a get together at my parent's house. Given the group of people I was hanging around, it was no surprise that by 10 p.m. I had thrown the last of my money in on an eight ball of coke, and suddenly lost any concern about the impending urine test I would have to provide the next morning.

The recruiter picked me up around 9 a.m. and brought me to the MEPS office. As planned, the first order of business was to provide a urine sample. Sure as hell when they stuck the test stick in it, I wasn't feeling confident that I was going to be raising my hand in the Oath of Enlistment that afternoon.

The very confused and angry recruiting staff member in charge of the urinalysis process turned around and said, "You got a ride out of here? You're not joining the Navy today."

This would be the first of the many disgraceful, low down, shameful positions that I would put myself in due to my drug use. My gut hit the floor, and I walked out of the MEPS office and called my parents.

"Not surprising." was the response I recall hearing on that phone call.

At this point it was pretty clear what I had been up to. I spent the better part of the last eight months staying out all night, sleeping all day and being broke just 48 hours after payday. All of the telltale signs of a coke addict. After the stint with my sister's car accident, and though none of it was seriously addressed, my parents were hip to the behaviors of stimulant addicts even in the midst of my dad's cancer treatment and mom's opiate nods.

Thinking back now, I wonder why I was never asked about treatment or wanting some kind of help. Not that I would have necessarily taken that step, but my sister was clearly having problems with substances and booze; alcoholism was prevalent in our family; mom was getting ridiculous amounts of narcotics prescribed and I'm over here beginning to fuck my life up.

I didn't do much of anything for the month following the flop at the MEPS office. My Dad on the other hand, hadn't given up on my entrance to the Navy, and asked the recruiter if there was another way around waiting a certain period of time before trying to enlist again.

By late May there was a recruiter from a separate office that had figured if I could just sign the paperwork and hold off on a military occupational choice, he could shove me off to boot camp within a week at best.

I think the most rigid my parents ever got with me was during the last week leading up to my second attempt at leaving for basic training. Almost no one came over to the house, and we went out to eat with close friends and family members. Other than drinking a few beers, I hadn't used any coke at all for about two or three weeks, which was probably the longest I had gone without it for the last eleven months. The last night home before leaving I hung out with my friends Ericka and Renny. It was a laid back evening and a nice send off, and sure was a far cry from my first try at enlistment.

I got up the following morning, well-rested and ready to go. I was nervous, yet actually excited for the unpredictable experience ahead. Any shakiness I had at the first go-around was gone, now that I knew I was going to be able to provide a negative UA at the MEPS office today. I finally felt like there was a sense of being and existence that lay ahead for me. I was about to be part of something that I could identify with every minute of my life. I would go to sleep and wake up a member of the armed services; a veteran, a sailor, for who knows how long. This was a sense of growing up and responsibility I had longed for.

I attended Navy boot camp from June to August 2002 in Great Lakes, Chicago, Illinois. To be honest, I loved everything about basic training. It wasn't the super hard-assed, in your face, Marine Corps boot camp, but it had its moments.

The US military thrives on its ability to take individuals in, some in need of structure and discipline, (like myself) break them down in each branch's own special way to accommodate it's needs, and build them out into useful resources. The structure and framework of basic training is to get everyone on the same page; no more individuality, no special circumstances. Sixty to seventy men live in a barracks, and everything is painted haze-gray like Navy ships. Two rows of double bunks, about 30-35 on each side, with shelves for stowage of clothing and supplies in between each set of bunks. Everybody does things the same way, at the same time of day, with the same supplies or equipment, and we went through the motions as a unit. We developed comradery, and the ability to count on one another. If one is unable to fall in line with the structure, they are called out, made an example of, and usually after one or two incidents of having your ass put on front-street in front of sixty other recruits, you manage to get your shit together.

One thing I have come to know to be true about my experience in the service, is that those of us that joined to escape some past life or came seeking structure and accountability, tend to gravitate towards one another. I feel like we never truly disconnect from the life that did not serve us; but I don't know, maybe some service members have. But in my reality, I always ended up very close to others with legal troubles or addictions, or challenging upbringings and home environments. I became tight with these guys Glover and Anthony, and both of their histories were very similar to mine. The structure during the day was great, but by the evenings, if we had some downtime, we were almost invariably discussing the "glory days" of our use and dysfunction.

I think this had some to do with the unknowing steps on the horizon and falling into a stagnant routine, which I would later learn is a compromising place once achieving some separation from substances. That sudden inability to bring into mind the recent disasters that came with my living a life revolved around substances was problematic. This would go on throughout the next three years in the Navy, and that gravitation toward people like me would eventually lead me out of the service in the same way I almost didn't make it in. I just didn't yet have the awareness of the old traps I would fall into.

For the most part, the days went by fairly easily. Other than the training grounds and barracks being hot as hell in the summer, one is easily worn out by nighttime. About halfway through my time in basic, I met with classification, or a job counselor. As mentioned, in order for me to ship out quickly I needed to agree to go to boot camp undesignated, or jobless. Leaving basic training undesignated typically lands individuals in the less desirable military occupations.

Being 19, unknowingly jingoistic rather than patriotic, and having been molded into the man the US armed forces needed me to be at that time, only one of the job offerings held my interest.

"Alright Conniff, so here's what's available: Hull Tech, Mess Specialist, undesignated deck department, or Aviation Ordnance." the classification guy said.

"What's ordnance?" I asked.

"Aviation warfare and explosives. Bombs and missiles, basically."

"Great." I said. "I'll take it."

"Don't you want to know more about it?" he asked.

"Not really, but now that you're asking, where's the school for it?" I asked

He looked over the paperwork then replied, "Pensacola, Florida."

"I'm in."

In response to 9/11, my role as an ordnance technician was to assist in the build-up and loading of aircraft weaponry that would contribute to many of the bombing operations in Iraq and Afghanistan in the years to come.

The 9/11 attacks were an absolute atrocity of course, and I think anyone can agree on that. But the ongoing "War on Terror" like most other wars, is a case of young men fighting old men's wars, and underpinning it all, is the almighty dollar and earthly resources, often blindly fought for in the name of freedom and democracy. With that said, it is easy to be misled and lifted up into a position of being told you are brave and courageous to fight against that which threatens the safety and freedom of one's homeland. I believe that somewhere, sometime, the United States has to stop injecting itself and its military into the politics of other nations.

I don't believe any informed citizen with an understanding of the workings of the military industrial complex would fight this country's wars for its leaders, knowing that they drag on for the years that they do due to the profit of war, and what the generational traumas and consequences of war are on families and cultures. The American way is, after centuries of looting and genocide of the Native populations and enslavement and oppression of Black people that we continue to overthrow, slaughter and destroy other lands and their inhabitants that do not look like us in skin color, and do not embrace our concept of freedom and democracy. This is the childish notion that perpetuates the disconnection that the experiences and lives of others are less valuable than ours here in the US. Because we are taught to disagree with the politics of other nations, say for instance socialism, many of us have been raised to believe that we are the greatest nation on the planet and to be subsequently in agreement with that we have to become strung out on indifference; driven by and addicted to quelling our fears of other political and economic systems at home and abroad, ultimately supporting US imperialism.

I too was one of these not so reasonably informed citizens that went on to pursue violence in the name of freedom and democracy, for blind love of my country. Today I don't agree with the person I was then, but I am grateful for finally understanding that confused young man. In my experiences, it was easy for me to blame others for the difficulties in the world; hell, I had already been taught that. The military was a perfect example and manifestation of my alcoholism and addiction feeding on external factors. There was no need to fight on the inside for freedom. The fight for freedom was going on overseas, and I was going to be a part of it.

So yes, at my age of misunderstanding, personal fears and gusto, I gladly took the job. I graduated basic training, had my parents and good friend Al come to see the graduation ceremony for one afternoon, and then they flew back to Massachusetts. Before military occupational school (or A-School as it's called in the

Navy) you are typically not permitted to travel home until after completion of the school.

I spent two months at the Naval Aviation Technical Training Center in Pensacola. Fortunately, I got roomed up with Anthony, and Glover was in the next barracks over. We spent a lot of our time playing cards in the dorms and using the amenities on the base. A lot of our conversations of drugs and the lifestyle began to fall away as we were beginning to align ourselves with our upcoming purpose in the fleet after schooling. Life in the world's greatest Navy. Making rank. Going on deployment, foreign ports, all of that. But hey, it worked. I was excelling in my classes and my parents were proud. I was also finally proud of myself.

For the first time in years, my grades would actually pay off. When it comes to A-School in the Navy, the best grades at the end of training gets the first picks on duty assignments. At this point, I was second in my class. First pick went to Torrey, another guy that was from basic who had the top grade. His choice, San Diego, was the only shore duty assignment on the whiteboard that morning besides Guam, in which case nobody in our class besides the instructors even knew where the hell that was. The list went on with line after line of ship names and hull numbers. Most were orders to ships homeported in Washington State and Virginia, or being attached to a flight squadron that would end up shipboard anyways.

"Hey Conniff you should pick the Truman, CVN-75, it's the newest aircraft carrier. That ship was just commissioned in '97!" a fleet returnee had piped up from the back of the class.

Since he had been shipboard already, what he had said carried a little more weight and knowledge in helping me choose. The Truman was homeported out of Norfolk, VA, and I started thinking about the times my old man said he used to drive guys back to Massachusetts on the weekends when he was stationed in Virginia during Korea.

"I'll take the Truman." I said.

A week later I flew into Logan airport in Boston. My old man picked me up, along with my cousin Chris and a couple of other friends. My father was so excited; I got off the flight in my uniform carrying my sea bag and other belongings. It was like his dreams had come true. The last kid in line; finally somebody joined the service, and I would go on to serve in the same branch and type of ship that he did some forty-five years earlier.

In retrospect, I had spent the previous couple of years leading up to basic training effectively learning to be an addict, and loathed what that had done to my self-esteem. When I say learning to be an addict, I mean learning to respond to life's difficulties by using. I didn't just use inexplicably; it wasn't a phenomenon of craving. I knew why I used and it was because using meant transforming the person I felt I was, into someone else. That someone else didn't feel the things Joe felt, or experience the world the way Joe did, at least while I was high. I learned that the process worked for me. No, it didn't last long, but it sure got me outside of being me, even for a little while. And suddenly with this newfound purpose and sense of duty, this is the first time ever that I could look at myself in the mirror and value and appreciate the person looking back at me without wanting to escape my skin in some capacity. I did drink during the trip home, but not like I needed it, and afterall drinking was surely part of stereotypical Navy culture as I understood it. I didn't use cocaine over the stay; and it didn't really cross my mind in the awe and excitement of being able to say that I had honestly become someone new after establishing myself in military life by completing boot camp.

I reported to Norfolk on Halloween of 2002, to find out my ship was out to sea doing a joint task force exercise. I remained on the base in a transitional barracks with my own room for about two weeks, and was only required to check in twice a week with a detailer. I had been told that I would await the return of the ship, and that we would be leaving for a six month deployment to the Mediterranean Sea by December. I spent most of my time in those weeks exploring the base and walking along the piers in amazement of the size of the naval ships docked there. The amount of people that came and went to work on those vessels while in port and all over the base was like watching a major city operating within itself.

One morning after chow, I made my way over to the check in desk, and the guy looked up and said, "Go get your stuff, they're flying you out to the ship later this morning."

I had roughly forty minutes to break down my linens and pack my sea bag. I recall thinking to myself, "What in the hell does 'flying out to the ship' look like?"

By 10:45 a.m. I was loaded into a little mail/parcel transport. Six of us sat rear facing in a little jet that was scheduled to take us to the ship. About an hour and a half into the flight, there was an announcement yelled from the front of the aircraft that we could see the ship out of the little windows.

The guy next to me looked over and said, "How the fuck are we going to land on that?'

It seemed impossible that this tiny transport was going to land safely on the flight deck of that ship. Nevertheless 120 mph and a few deep breaths later, the plane came to a halt. It's extremely unusual to land rear-facing and being stopped suddenly by a catch wire on an aircraft carrier.

As they began to unload us it was absolute chaos on the flight deck. Everyone was yelling over the noise of jet engines and steam catapults, throwing our bags out of the plane, and running us across the deck and down into a catwalk seventy-five feet above the water to get us inside the ship. It's an awfully strange experience.

Once inside the skin of the ship, a Lieutenant approached us and said, "Welcome aboard the USS Harry S. Truman."

6

Military Life

It took almost a month and a half before I got accustomed to finding my way around the ship. And within a week of gaining some confidence on my whereabouts around the boat, we left for a six month deployment.

Shipboard life is really something else, to say the least. We had about 6,000 people on our ship, once the aircraft squadrons were onboard. There were two ship stores; two gyms; a library; a chapel; food available twenty-three hours a day; and plenty of work to go around. The shifts out to sea went from six to six and you were either on nights or days. I managed to stay on days during my entire time in the Navy, and preferred it that way. I got to enjoy waking up in the morning to viewing the sunrise out through the hangar bay doors, and watched the sunsets at the end of my shift.

Most of all, what I really appreciated at this time was the structure that deployment offered. For one, I rarely thought about drugs or alcohol. I had purpose and I had community; I felt needed and valued. I was saving money and traveling and getting into a workout routine. I had a sense of brotherhood, and we had the ability to get to know each other quickly and efficiently while out to sea. This was the first time I remember that I was genuinely getting to know people without the need to dumb down my senses to let them into my life. We were all sharing something in common; our time and energy, and we had all made the sacrifice of family and friends to be of service to our country. I told myself this is what I was going to do for the next twenty years.

That first deployment was a Mediterranean cruise, so my port of calls consisted of Christmas in France, New Years in Crete, and my February birthday in Slovenia. On the way back, we spent three days in England, and I got to get an overnight in London with two friends. All in all I had truly incredible experiences, and I was not a mess during the port visits, even seemingly more responsible than some of my shipmates in a few cases. There is something to be said about not being able to "hold your booze" after two or three months at sea then swilling beer on an empty stomach, which I've seen become irresponsible and dangerous. Overall, I didn't feel the need to be totally wasted every time we walked off the ship. I knew that I would be back a few days later, leaving port with a job and a purpose, needed on the team. Plus I wanted to take in local culture and see landmarks while on some of the port visits.

Being part of the ordnance crews out to sea was a mix of operating weapons elevators, bringing bombs and missiles up and down from the magazines; standing watch, or helping with weapons support equipment. In port, the days were mostly spent around the hangar bay weapons shop and standing armed watches on the flight deck for four hours at a time with an M-16 or other firearm. Regardless of the task, I felt like I had so much responsibility while I was in the Navy. I had keys to weapons lockers, $3500 dollar hand-radios, and a gun card that allowed me to check out almost any weapon in the ship's armory and keep me accountable for the safety and security of those living on the ship.

When we finally returned to the US after six months, I couldn't wait to go home. I had a bunch of money saved, and it had been almost eight months since I had seen my family or friends.

After the first few days back in Massachusetts of attending dinners and getting together with family, I started hitting the town going out to clubs and such with friends. I wore my uniform when and wherever possible; I was proud and felt like I departed on such short notice months earlier that I wanted to show off that I had become someone.

After a week home, I rolled through the neighborhood Dunkin Donuts parking lot one evening and bumped into a friend of my ex Nicole's from high school. I hadn't seen her in a couple of years, and it was nice to bump into someone from that time, also considering I hadn't had any female companionship in over a year. Monica and I had not known each other really well, but she had been over at Nicole's a handful of occasions when I was there, and we knew many of the same people. She was really attractive; shorter than me, shoulder length bleached blonde hair and petite.

"Joe is that you?" she asked.

"Yeah, hey, how've you been? It's been a long time."

I walked over to the car, chatted for a few, and within minutes, we had plans to get together a couple nights later. I was scheduled to pick her up at her parent's place, and we were going to my buddy Matt's for a small social gathering.

We spent that night out getting caught up, talking about the last couple of years, and getting pretty lit to top it off. Eventually we ended up back at my parent's place in the spare room in the basement, and a relationship developed out of that evening.

I had to get back to Virginia about four days later, but we were committed to staying connected. This would begin the process of me making trips back and forth to Massachusetts on the weekends, just like my father did.

A week after I got back to Norfolk, most of my friends were just getting back from their leave time and it seemed everybody was getting new cars. We all had some money saved up, and if you've ever been anywhere near a military installation, there are usually handfuls of car dealerships ready to prey on returning service members offering them Camaros and Mustangs, and whatever else speaks to a twenty something year old with a steady paycheck and a little money down.

I bought a Mitsubishi Galant, and within a week was driving back home to see Monica for a weekend. This went on for a couple months, and occasionally I would bring a buddy along from the ship to come up, hang out and share the drive time.

One particular weekend I was headed back by myself. Not even the first five minutes that I rode into my hometown after the eight hour drive, I ran into my old skate buddy Dan at the gas station.

"Hey man, I heard you've been kicking it with Monica?"

"Yeah, yeah. How did you hear about that?" I asked.

"She runs with some of the same people I do; and believe me, you don't want to get tied up with her. Things around here are pretty bad with heroin and she's up in it." he said.

"Are you sure?" I asked.

"Yeah, it hasn't been long, but do yourself a favor and don't get caught up." he said.

This was interesting because he wasn't doing too hot either. He didn't look well, but he and I went way back and I trusted him.

"Alright man, thanks. Good to see you."

He nodded his head and said, "Yeah you too."

I think initially I was in a state of denial, but come to think of it, I hadn't really been in her presence for full days. So honestly, I really had no way of knowing for sure.

By now I had moved in with a couple of other guys from the ship. We got an apartment right up the street from the base, and it became kind of a crash pad for our buddies that got too drunk on the way back to the ship.

The hard facts were that the guys I was staying with all had extensive histories with substance use before the Navy. Imagine that, I was gravitating right back towards people with similar experiences hoping to be around folx I felt truly understood me. I believe this had much to do with us not being out to sea with deeper purpose and levels of commitment, and a whole lot of spare time.

None of this initially started out with drugs in the mix, but there was plenty of heavy drinking. Many days we only worked from roughly seven in the morning until Noon, so regardless if it was 10 a.m. or 2 p.m. and we were done with work and off the ship, it would generally be considered a good time to start drinking. A handful of our buddies had gotten their own places scattered around Norfolk, so there was always a place to kick back and for those of us not yet of age, someone to buy alcohol.

I continued to make my trips home to see Monica, and it quickly became clear that she was using. At this time, I really didn't know a whole lot about heroin outside of my experiences with Jose, except that people that used it had typically started on Oxycontin, and when that became more regulated it was straight to the street dope. Once that happened it was like the point of no return for many people I grew up with. My hometown had experienced OD's in the previous years, resulting in deaths of a handful of people I went to school with, but by 2003 the opioid crisis was really starting to take flight in Agawam.

I think part of my unwillingness to actually dig deeper with the truth of Monica's use was brought on by the reality that I was slowly slipping back into my own patterns of behavior with drinking, and the more I did that, the more I thought about cocaine. Confirming that Monica was using heroin was an intimidating thought. I never saw needles, or any paraphernalia for that matter, so I allowed myself the room to write off the severity of it all.

Eventually though, the truth came out; she casually said she was using it and that it was pretty cheap, but that she wanted to stop. She was sniffing pure dope and scoring it with all of these other people I knew and grew up with.

This gave me an in to my relationship with her to start messing around with coke again when I would come home for the weekends. The more and more I let the reality of her using slide, the further I dug into calling my old dealers on the trips home or buying blow from her contacts. To be honest, my being high on my chosen substance offered some reprieve from the impending doom of a relationship with Monica addicted to heroin.

I don't want to come across as if minimizing the use of cocaine over heroin, but to be truthfully speaking from my direct experiences, opiates require so much more attention than cocaine does from start to finish each day. Addiction doesn't really take days off, but heroin sure as hell doesn't miss a beat. Monica's addiction to heroin would become my addiction to the chaos of her need for it and the desire for me to medicate myself while helping her figure out how to stay well. Our relationship was the perfect storm.

Everyone thought I was crazy for getting involved with her; but it gave me a sense of being and purpose again. And after all the events in past relationships, I considered her true to me, which was not really the case but that was the feeling I was experiencing. I felt like she truly wanted to be with me, and I looked right past all the shit that came with that dynamic for the small sense of value I received.

Back in Virginia, the binge drinking in our apartment had progressed to extreme alcoholism rapidly. Quickly the group I was hanging with in Norfolk was getting bored with the drinking by 7-8 p.m. and we were starting to get connected to a few people that could get us other stuff. Pretty soon, there were mushrooms, ecstasy, and finally a steady stream of cocaine available within our circle. We had connections who weren't fully aware of our military occupations, and one of the dealers sold about three to five different substances on any given Friday, which gave us a real sense of grab bag excitement of what the state of disorientation would look like by 1 a.m. Saturday morning.

One of the weekends my buddy Tommy and I decided to visit both of our hometowns in one trip. He and I shared one of the bedrooms at the apartment, and we wanted to get a change of scenery for the weekend. We passed through his hometown near Scranton, Pennsylvania and then headed on to Massachusetts for two days. In our absence, our friend Kevin had asked if he could crash in our room while we were gone, and we agreed that it would be alright.

Late Sunday morning, while we were in Massachusetts, Tommy got a call. I saw the look on his face and I immediately knew something fucked up had happened.

Tommy finally began talking, "Ok we'll start heading back now. We'll be there in about nine hours. Where is he now?" there was a short pause, and then he said, "Ok, we'll be there when we can." and Tommy hung up.

He got up quickly, looking about and said, "Kevin shot himself."

"What? What the fuck? At our house? Are you serious? You asked where he was.... he's alive?" I asked.

Tommy shrugged and said, "Yeah, somehow. I didn't get details, but he's at the hospital."

Once we were finally on the road, we started getting more info about what actually happened. Kevin and one other roommate, David, were the only ones at our place Saturday night, which seemed totally out of the ordinary, but they both had duty section on Sunday and needed to be on the ship early, so they told everyone to split and not hang out.

Both of the guys had been drinking as usual, but Kevin on the other hand, had a disagreement with his girlfriend over the phone, and got pretty bent. Jägermeister was the common shot drink at our house and Kevin had a real affinity for it. Based on what David said, Kevin had put away the better part of a half-gallon, mostly on his own, and then David crashed out for the night. When he got up to get Kevin ready for duty the next morning, as he walked out of his room into the hall, he noticed blood spots all over the floor. He opened our door, and when he walked in, the pistol was on the bed and Kevin was laying there, apparently having woken up in the middle of the night to take a piss (after shooting himself) and went and passed back out. Once David realized what had happened, he called the duty section leader and told him they had an emergency and wouldn't make it for morning muster. He woke Kevin, got him into his car and sped off to the nearest hospital.

By the time we got back to the hospital in Norfolk, Kevin was awake. Basically he got super smashed, argued with his lady (not sure which came first) and then stuffed his .45 pistol to Tommy's pillow held against his face and pulled the trigger. David had been so hammered he passed out and never heard it, nor did any of the neighbors. The whole thing was unbelievable.

When Tim and I went home, our bedroom looked like a crime scene. Tommy's bed was covered in blood, and there were pieces of tissue and whatever else came out of Kevin's face on the wall between our beds. The bullet had passed through the back side of his mouth closer to his cheek, ripped through the wall, through the copper shower pipe in the bathroom, and the remainder of the projectile was laying in the bathtub.

All of it was traumatizing in its own right. It was damn near impossible to believe anybody walked away, based on the looks of our room. Tommy and I spent the following two days after work cleaning the blood off of our wall, and Kevin was required by our department to complete an inpatient substance use program off-base, and that seemed to be the last anyone heard of it.

After the incident anybody known to hang at our apartment was under close watch from the higher ups in our division. Before long, I was getting a lot of shit from my chief petty officer about smelling like booze, and after a time where I came to the ship late twice in one week, he recommended me for an inpatient alcohol treatment program. I didn't really fight it, and my career was on the line. I needed a break from the apartment, and the weekend trips to Massachusetts were so out of hand trying to keep up with the rollercoaster of Monica's heroin use. After the whole thing with Kevin, none of us had slowed our partying. You'd think we'd tone it down a bit but our young, military culture was just work hard, play hard. It wasn't like the vibes in our household suddenly took a turn for the better; having a friend try to kill himself in your bedroom really does something to fuck with the energy of your space.

I went to a thirty day intensive program on the base, and was in with a lot of guys from other branches that were struggling with chemical dependence. Some were on their way out for disciplinary measures taken related to their use, and a handful were given another chance, like in my case. We went to AA meetings out in town four nights a week and did group programming during the day. I was really interested in the comradery of the twelve step programs, given there was this group of people excited about their lives without drinking. Honestly though, at 21 years old I found it difficult to wrap my head around the idea of giving up something I had just legally turned of age to do.

We had one on ones and group therapy sessions which I started to see some benefit from. The Bill Gates looking counselor assigned to me started uncovering some of the shit I had experienced around substance use in my home and dug into the relational challenges I had faced. It just didn't feel safe to discuss the current battle with Monica and her heroin use; I was already skating on thin ice. I did feel like there was a lot being gained by just talking to somebody about how I felt, and it became clear I wasn't used to having somebody be reflective in their listening to me, validating my feelings.

My dad made the trip down for the completion of the program, and upon returning to my apartment, lifestyle and friends, I was drunk again within three days.

My trips to Massachusetts started up again regularly, but now once I got into town, I never knew where the hell Monica would be. I remember a couple of occasions speaking with her as I got off of the freeway into New York City, only two hours away, and she would be waiting at her place. But by the time I would get to town she would be up in Springfield, in project buildings doped up, and I'd have to get her to my car. In all of this I somehow convinced myself I was in love with this person. In actuality I was just attached to the idea of what this person represented missing from my life: companionship. This wasn't a relationship, it was transactional. This was using and abusing of drugs and each other, with some decent sex trickled in.

From my experience, military life does disastrous things to the young person's mind's conception of love and relationship dynamics. I mean who the fuck doesn't come home from six months out to sea or a year in Afghanistan in hopes that they will have someone to come home to? I know that's how I felt, especially in conjunction with my feelings of being unlovable or some other insecurity from the past. This was at least giving me some semblance of being involved with somebody, no matter how toxic it was.

To make matters worse, we decided it would be a good idea to get married. We relied on each other so much, and having someone make that official was somehow going to make it work in the long run, or so we thought. Our families tried to walk us back from the idea at first; but in the long run no one was successful in deterring us. Then there's also the possibility that not one of our families knew any better about how to handle this situation. I mean my family wasn't well versed in healthy relationship characteristics, and her family had plenty of chaos with her older sister's relationship and the grandchildren at home and all that came with that. Her father was quick to honor the marriage, perhaps with hopes we would make a healthy life somewhere. For the last couple of years they had been coexisting with her heroin addiction in hopes something would help to break her free.

We had a Jack' n Jill celebration so both our friends and families could meet each other. It probably won't come as a surprise that we were late arriving to our own gathering put on by our families because we were trying to make sure we had enough drugs for us both to get through the evening. Late to our own party; addicts do shit like that.

We got married at a park a few weeks later. Just our parents and my godfather, and then we went on to get a cheap motel for a honeymoon evening. I ran out of coke and booze earlier than expected, and watched her nod off for the rest of the night; only to have us argue about how to get money for drugs the following morning.

By the time my next six month deployment was within sight, Monica had moved into the spare room at my parent's house, and I was still using coke on the weekends whether I was in Virginia or Massachusetts, but with an upcoming out to sea period, I was shifting to getting focused on work again. I knew the structure would be good for me, and I had some high hopes that adding responsibility to her like the car payment and helping my parents out would help her begin to see past the idea of staying high every day. How little I knew about how having expectations and addiction travel together.

Leading up to deployment, our ship was still in port for repairs. As we prepared ourselves and ship spaces, I became really close with another guy from Massachusetts that was also on board the ship, Chris. It was almost as if he was tasked out to work with me and help me keep my shit together. He was on me like glue, along with a new supervisor, Jason. I think that they both saw my potential, yet neither knew very much about the chaotic nature of my personal life outside of my drinking that brought on the need for extra supervisory attention.

Chris had an apartment, wife and child on the way. He had the kind of life that I aspired to, but felt I really had little hope of achieving. I started spending more time with him, and less with the other fellas. His friendship helped me remain centered and grounded in showing up for myself and goals around the Navy, so long as I was close to him.

The thought of leaving Monica in Massachusetts while I went on a six month cruise was really wearing me down, not so much because of being away from her, but because I really felt things weren't changing for the better. She was spending more time with people I never met, always around dealers, and who the hell knows what she was doing for the drugs. All I know is any money I was sending home was never enough.

Three months into the deployment we had passed through the Suez Canal, and the back pay from the marriage hit, and I got about $9,000 deposited overnight. I was beginning to think that there was a future with financial security ahead. Realistically though, when I tried to call from the shipboard phones, she was never home. My father was expressing his dissatisfaction with the whole situation of her living there.

During the previous deployment, my friend Amy had spent a lot of time over at my folk's place helping out. She would cook breakfast, hang out with my mom, just making herself available for conversation, that kind of thing. This go around with Monica was a tremendous shift in energy in their home. My dad also mentioned that the money that was supposed to go to the car payments wasn't, and he was receiving notices in the mail of potential repossession if they didn't receive the balance soon.

Finally, the day came when my chief pulled me into the office after a port visit overseas.

As he slammed the door he said, "Conniff, what the fuck is going on with your finances? Why do we have creditors reaching out to the command asking about why you're not paying your bills?"

"Chief, can you give me more information? I'm not clear as to what bills you're referring to?" I said.

"Your car payment, a 1999 Mitsubishi. They are trying to find it for repossession. You need to handle your shit Conniff. Straighten this out somehow." he demanded.

"Yes chief, I'm on it."

Two days later I was able to connect with my Dad and came to find out he had already taken matters into his own hands.

Monica hadn't been back home to my folk's place in a couple of weeks since I brought the repossession notice to her attention.

"Joe, here's what's going on. I took the spare key and went with a couple guys and found your car. It was down off Plainfield Street. There were burnt spoons, needle caps and empty baggies all over the car. What do you want me to do?" he asked.

I took a breath, thought for a second and said, "Call the loan agency and tell them to come get the car. And let me speak to her."

"I don't know where she is," he said.

I hung up the phone, took off my wedding band and decided that I could only focus on myself and whatever I needed to do to not lose what I had left going for me with the Navy. She didn't have access to any more money unless I sent it to her, and I wasn't going to continue to do that since the car wasn't being paid for. I had given her a couple thousand dollars over the last few months, what I thought would have been enough to cover the car and plenty of walking around cash for herself and habit.

There were upcoming exams for rank promotion in March, and Chris and I spent all of our work downtime studying together, and after working hours we were at the shipboard gym. I was ready to return home, make rank and move on with shit, with or without her. I focused the remaining months preparing for the test and enjoying port visits with Jason and Chris, trying to build a new circle.

As we all started preparing for our return home, my parents let me know that Monica had started coming back around, and that she was clean. She wanted to come to see the return of the ship and spend a few days together, with my folks and her mom.

I agreed, but I wasn't 100% sold on how this relationship was going to continue.

When we pulled back into homeport, we spent a few days around town, and then all flew back to Massachusetts together. The disconnection between us was growing, and I really didn't know how to handle the dynamic after what went down with the car and finances while I was gone. We were now different people without the familiar chaos.

I felt lost again. I had found a renewed purpose out to sea with Chris and admired his direction and attention to his career and family, especially after I made a commitment to focus on myself out to sea. I had an overwhelming obligation to this person that I no longer knew. And yeah, she was no longer using and was on methadone. But this was not the person I married. You have to understand just because someone is sober does not mean that the relationship is easier or better; things become extremely challenging. I was also trying not to engage in drinking or drugging, but without the substances we were both raw, damaged individuals that knew nothing about the communication of our feelings or needs.

Everything we ever felt or desired was met with a line of coke or hit of dope; that leveled the playing field for us both. With the absence of narcotics we were like opposite magnetic poles being forced to rub up against one another because of our marriage, but being driven apart by the unseen inner turmoil that existed. I was 22, and she was 20. People our age didn't have things like marriage or relationship counseling in our vocabulary, partly because many people understand that's just not a wise time to get married, for starters.

Finally the news came. I had passed the exam, first increment. This meant I would begin getting paid immediately, typically before I would get my new rank sewn onto my uniforms. The rate exam consisted of a 200 question test and when my results came in, 198/200 were correct.

This is a reminder of how successful I am able to be in a structured environment. I was a section leader in boot camp; I excelled in A-school to finish second in my class, and now these test results. But as of right now, I had lost my inner compass and outer support. Chris was on leave with his family that first week I came back from Massachusetts and I was drawn back into drinking with the old crew almost immediately.

A few of us went out to celebrate the exam results by bar hopping at Virginia Beach and ending up at a random party by 11 p.m. A few of the people I was with scored some blow, and without batting an eye, I threw down $20 and asked for a quick hook up to keep me going with the night of drinking.

As soon as I got my coke, I did what I bought and immediately drove off high into my own world for the next couple hours. I was already feeling the sense that even though I had just achieved some success, I wasn't deserving of the happiness and celebration because I have the tendency to let everyone down, including myself. And that's exactly what I was doing: self-sabotaging.

Internally and deep down, I knew I was more of a drug addict than I was a sailor in the US Navy. I didn't want to be the addict, I wanted to be the sailor. That's the catch. But realistically, given the feelings of disconnection and overwhelming events that required attention in my personal life, I was going to get relief the only way I knew how, and I needed to do it now, tonight. The coke wouldn't have been there if I didn't need to do it, that's the way I viewed things.

When I finally came down about 2 a.m. I parked my car at the off-base lot and got a taxi to an acquaintance's apartment on the base for a bit before making my way onto the ship for morning muster.

When I walked onto the ship, I crossed paths with one of my supervisors in the hangar bay.

"Hey Conniff, heads up, command urinalysis sweep is going on today. Make sure you drop a sample before you leave the ship for the afternoon." he said, as he grabbed the door handle and turned into the office.

I fucking choked on my insides. I don't even know if I said anything else to him other than make eye contact and give him a nod.

A UA, today? I had never been called for a UA on the ship; not once. Talk about fate, destiny or whatever you want to call it, but everything was caving in on me at that very moment.

And all I could think about was how I needed to get off the ship and call that guy that gave me the coke last night, so I could get some more and forget about all of this that was happening. Just for a little while, only then I could figure out how to handle everything that was about to come crashing down.

I went down to the UA lines, dropped my sample, and went and hit my rack. I laid there thinking about how long it might take for the results to come back and the command to process me out of the Navy. I called my parents and told them what was about to happen; I wasn't positive how long it would take, but it was just a matter of time.

My father said, "Joe, I'm not angry with you. I'm just really disappointed."

Have you ever been told by a parent that "they're disappointed?" Somehow to me, that shit hurts so much worse than receiving a parent's anger. I actually wanted him to be angry. I felt like maybe his anger would have spoken more to me in the sense of "Are you done with this shit yet? Haven't drugs continuously fucked up your life and only made it more difficult?" I needed to hear that more. Would that have changed anything? Not likely, but to me his response felt more like "It was just a matter of time" or "we knew this was coming". My parents had more predictability of what drugs were doing to my life than I did, and that's a damn shame.

That UA happened in late April, and I was processed out and back in Massachusetts as a civilian by the first week of July 2005.

7

Happy

After the arraignment on May 5th I was released. Somehow I managed to blow enough smoke to my newly assigned drug court case manager about some random shelter housing opportunity I had heard about that they decided to PR me, under the condition that I show back up next Monday morning for drug court orientation.

It was only Tuesday.

Here's the biggest challenge I see serving any time in downtown King County jail. It doesn't make a difference if you've had five days or five months to dry out there, when you get released, you get let out to Fifth Avenue and James Street.

Fifth and James is in the central business district of Seattle. The only place someone walking out of custody fits in or is welcome downtown is two blocks west at 3rd and James.

Downtown Emergency Service Center (DESC) operates the old Morrison Hotel at 3rd and James, which happens to be directly across the street from King County Superior Court. The Morrison provides services and housing to Seattle residents facing homelessness, MH and SUD challenges, and has extensive drug activity and violence in the surrounding blocks.

With that said, when you exit the jail in crisis and just want a cigarette, you go to the corner by the entrance to the Morrison. This is the edge of "here we go again" for some of us. Ten blocks north of The Morrison is the Blade, where I was arrested almost two weeks prior. What new tools does an individual have that goes into custody, sits for one or two weeks, and is then released to the same relative area in which they were arrested? None.

I had no home to go to and I had burnt every bridge over these last months. I was an absolute disgrace to my daughter in my own mind, and I couldn't get anyone to post ten percent of $1000 bail. By now, my family was sapped on resources and patience with my addiction. My mom threw her last $20 on for commissary in the jail, and I only had $5 and some change that booking/release cashed me out with. The only thing I really had going for me was that my food stamp card was loaded while I was in custody; $196 for the month, which translates to $98 on the streets. But all I really wanted to do was get a pizza and soda from 711, sit my ass down, and figure out where to stay and how to not use so I wouldn't get caught up again before the drug court orientation Monday morning.

"Hey man, did you just get out?" said the familiar voice.

As I turned around, I recognized Val from The Blade. We rarely ran together, but we had done a deal or two with each other in the previous months.

"Yep." I responded, lighting up a smoke I bought off a stranger.

"How long were you in?" asked Val.

"Not long, just short of two weeks. All part of the arrests from that sweep."

Val looked around at some of the passersby and said, "Yeah, you won't even recognize it up there on the block. They moved the main bus pick up straight off the Blade and down a block and a half to thin the foot traffic, then they took out the newspaper stands and benches too."

The newspaper stands served as a make-shift kiosk to buy dope; rather than walking down the street and having to keep looking over your shoulder for the police. At the stands you might have six or seven bodies gathered and conversing around two newspaper bins, making it easy to do hand to hand deals without having a lookout.

"So whatcha gonna do now?" he asked.

"Shit, I really don't know. I just gotta get by 'til Monday and get to this drug court orientation in the morning, maybe come up with some kind of plan once that gets rolling. I have this other case out of day reporting that needs me to show up as well, same day."

"For real? You're gonna give it a try?" he asked, looking puzzled.

"I don't know, I mean shit, I need to. What can anybody put together out here? My old man is really sick down in Cali, and I just missed my daughter's birthday at the beginning of last month. Even though it was in jail, this is the most clean time I've had in years. What about you? What do you have going on?"

"Man, with all the dope being driven off the block, I've found this new guy up in Queen Anne, sells $60 grams. I've been going through him and trying to move a little bit around to stay well."

"$60 grams huh, that's pretty good. Decent shit?" I asked.

"Yep, real good."

Until now, I had been thinking about that pizza and pop from 711, but not as hard as I was now thinking about those $60 grams.

Within the next ten minutes, I had made the decision to get the pizza and soda, but I was going to take that food stamp card straight to Twelfth and Jackson right after, flip that around (basically illegally selling the value for fifty cents on the dollar) to get that $90 cash and go with Val to Queen Anne, and buy a gram and some baggies. I thought I would use just a little of it to get my head straight and have some pocket money, and I can figure out a shelter or something for the next few days.

We jumped on the next number seven bus that rolled by the Morrison and took care of the food stamp flip in Little Saigon, all in the course of forty-five minutes and then caught the bus to Queen Anne.

Val's guy came through right on time; and the gram was fat too. I probably smoked three points of the H in Queen Anne, gave Val two and he went about his business. I sold a couple by the waterfront and the urge for some coke arose, so there I was again. Within three hours after my release I was coming out of the alley behind Target with only three points of black left and $20 of crack. Same shit, different week; and the whole idea of making it to orientation and day reporting went up in dope smoke in the alley behind the Showbox.

I managed to move myself and little bits of dope around the downtown corridor for the next week.

The following Thursday evening I had run into Shorty and Gerard on Western Ave. A friend of theirs was letting them crash in his shop over in White Center. He was coming to pick them up, and I could come along if I wanted to.

Shorty and Gerard were these older Mexican guys I knew that were into moving boosted shit around, like perfume, cologne and 501 jeans. These were the cats you went to if you had hot items and needed to turn it into cash or drugs quickly.

"You got any dope?" I asked Gerard.

"Yeah, a little bit, maybe enough to get the three of us through 'til tomorrow morning, that's it though. Then we'll have to figure something out." he said.

"Cool, cool. I've got about $17 bucks. I'll take a point and a half and save some bus fare to get back to the city tomorrow.

After fifteen minutes of sitting around talking about what we could do for tomorrow's money, this 1980's something, beat up brown Buick Regal pulled up. The three of us got in and we rolled off towards the West Seattle bridge and over to White Center.

When we got to the garage, it became clear that these guys had their damn tent set up inside the shop.

The funniest part about it all is that there were a couple small couches and chairs worth crashing on, but this is the thing I've learned about folx that spend time living out of doors or on the streets: they are quite particular about their set-ups, especially their tents, bed rolls and so on. These guys were committed to how they did things, and that provided them with the same sense of security and safety most of us know that get to close our gates and lock our doors at night.

By the time I nodded off for good it had to have been late, and I woke up somewhere around 10 a.m. For a while there it was hard for me to get more than seven or eight hours of sleep a night, mostly due to my use, and my body would usually wake in the discomfort of needing heroin. I had just spent the last eight days running laps around downtown trying to sell and buy dope and being spun out on crack, so this was the first night I wasn't curled up in some doorway being moved along at sunrise by the downtown city workers or Seattle PD. The shit part about being a heroin addict is you can be separated from the stuff for a couple weeks, come back to it, and within two days, be right back up to where you left off.

When I stumbled out of the garage, I realized that on the way there I hadn't paid any attention to where in White Center we were, so not only did I feel like garbage, I now had to figure out where the nearest bus stop was to get back to the city. This was actually a nice neighborhood, and I felt like hot trash trying to walk my despicable self out of it.

After about twenty minutes I found the stop for the next bus to downtown. Before I left, I stole an unopened bottle of cologne from their stockpile to flip when I got back to the city. I had just enough fare for the bus, and the cologne would get me enough cash to get well.

When I jumped off the bus, I damn near tripped over Omar's foot. This is perfect; I knew he would be interested in a bottle of cologne. This was one of his hustles besides running around selling dope with two older guys. He was from Bahrain, and was a few years younger than me; a super nice guy. He helped me out towards the end before the bust, giving me a place to crash for a few days, and I set him up with old man Mark as a connection. Omar was renting by the week up on Aurora, and always had unopened cologne and perfume laying around his room.

Sure as hell, he took it off my hands, gave me the $10, and I ran across the street to catch one of the guys I knew. T was moving in a hurry with Keith, and I figured this was my best chance to score in the daytime with the ongoing full court press from the police.

Things were lining up nicely. T said they were just headed up to meet their guy in front of Benaroya Hall and I could throw my cash in. After that we would roll up to Freeway Park and get right.

It was a beautiful day. Friday afternoon, mid-May, the weather was pretty warm. We pulled out our dope, and all sat down to do our thing at some tucked away steps by Madison Street.

Keith got up first to move around a bit, and before the look on his face registered to me something was wrong, I saw a little red dot on his chest.

"Drop the shit and step towards the wall." the voice said.

I slowly put my foil and lighter down, turned around and saw a cop with his taser pointed in our direction.

"Let's be clear, this can be easy and everyone can walk out of here if your names check out clean. Throw the dope in the trash, step on the paraphernalia. Pull out your wallets, or whatever kind of ID you have, one at a time. Ok, you two, sit down while I start with him." the officer said.

Keith pulled out a beat up wallet, rifled through it and said, "I ain't got any ID."

The officer said, "Ok, name, date of birth and last known address."

Keith spouted off some bullshit name and other info, and after two minutes of radio chatter, he checked out. Boom; off he goes. T gives him his ID, and somehow comes out clean too, and he leaves.

As all of this was unfolding, my insides started to shift. I felt tired. Not tired like "I had a long fucking day tired", but the kind of tired that says, "I absolutely can't live another day like this, in this skin". The tired that stares you in the face and says, "this is the only fucking break you'll get if you keep on doing what you're doing, a couple weeks or years behind bars if this shit keeps piling up." I started to feel like going to jail right now would bring more relief than another delusional day living out here on the streets, trying to get the medicine just right so I don't have to think or feel. Maybe it's even prison now, given I dodged and went on warrant.

I had my head down thinking through the consequences in between coming and going on the dope high, and then there was some radio chatter. All I heard was scratches and fuzzies and "warrant", and then some more scratches and more talk of "warrant".

"Mr. Conniff, you know what's going to happen next right?"

"Sure do." I put my hands behind my back, heard the cuffs come out and felt my wrists get closer, and we walked to the blue SUV.

I remember sitting in the back seat for what seemed like an hour. It was as if this guy could sense what I was going through and gave me ten minutes alone to think things through. I don't want to make this sound like I was suddenly sold on getting sober. Nope. I had no fucking idea how that would happen. But I really felt like anything could be better than going through this bullshit process again. Anything. It was almost as if this officer knew this was going to be my last high for a long time, and he would let me enjoy it for a few before another booking at the county jail.

All the pieces of my life that I had stopped showing up for; my daughter, my parents, family, myself, started washing over me with a sense of ease, compounded with the opiate high. All of it felt close for once; if I could just stay separated from drugs and alcohol for a reasonable period of time, maybe some kind of peace would be within reach. I could see my dad before he passed. I could see my daughter, even in custody before the other shoe drops with these warrants and I get hauled off for 12-24 months. Anything has to be better than this life I've been living.

There's something extremely defeating in wanting to affect change in one's life, but not having or understanding the means to do so. Right now, this is where I was in the back of that SUV. Regarding my addiction, every decision made and experience I've had has shaped my life right up until this moment. To me, this doesn't mean that someone who is strung out isn't responsible or doesn't play a part in their getting better; but how do we do it? For some of us, our "systems", or complex of behaviors that truly make up our addictions tend to have been in place for long periods of time. So the idea of committing to a diversion court model, or 30-60 day detox program seems fucking baffling, given the nature of trying to make it through a day of staying well and finding some kind of shelter. For some, staying well doesn't just mean not being dope sick, but rather getting enough of our substance for the right lift off from reality. Heroin definitely wasn't always mine, but as of recent it was really doing the job.

After another three hours of booking at the county jail, intertwined with watching the Prison Rape Elimination Act (PREA) video roughly fifty times, I got brought back up to the Tenth floor. Since there weren't any breakthroughs in my well-being, I didn't see the sense in making a phone call to anyone at the moment. I imagined once the courts had figured out what to do with me and the warrants, there may be some news worth sharing with my family. Until then, I might as well try to sleep it off for another day and a half and go through the motions of being in withdrawal all over again.

Finally the day came to go to court for the hearing. The good news is I actually now had over a week to dry out, and the last runner hadn't been too long, so I felt clear headed going into court this time. Still though, I had my suspicions on abilities to commit to a program as intensive as drug court, and given my release and immediate going on the run, I wasn't even sure if they were willing to work with me anymore. From what I understood, the program was supposed to be somewhere around a year long and I hadn't yet shown interest or commitment.

When they brought us into the bullpen to wait for our hearings, I started looking around for familiar faces. Finally one jumped out at me. I couldn't remember his name, but I felt I knew him from one of my brief stays in county back in February.

I popped a seat down pretty close to where he was and he immediately looked over and said, "Connor, right?"

"Yeah man, what's your name again? It's been a while."

Connor was a misunderstanding of my last name over the years that I started using on the street with some folx so people wouldn't know my real last name.

He gave a little grin and said, "Happy. Do you remember me from county a few months back?"

"No shit, that is you. Man you look really different, but good; you look healthy." I said.

The last time I saw Happy we ended up in the same pod on the ninth floor for a week or two, and we got to know each other pretty well. He was in on some older charges he caught, and hadn't been out of custody for some time. Back then his hair was scraggly, he looked like he had some weight displaced in an unhealthy sort of way; but to be honest, I probably currently looked similar to the way he did then.

After the first couple of days kicking dope in our own personal hells, some guy came to the unit that we knew from the streets and he had snuck in some crystal, so we spent an afternoon snorting that and chatting up our life stories. By the time we got moved to separate pods, we knew quite a bit about each other.

Happy said, "Thanks man, things are pretty good. What about you? You look like you're getting your ass torn up by the life out there."

"Yeah man I am!" I said, chuckling a bit. "They got me wrapped up in the downtown Crosstown Traffic bust, and they released me to drug court, but I ran again. Didn't make it a week this time."

"Yeah that's where they got me; picked me up downtown on delivery. I waited those couple months to get drug court, and shit man, it's a really good program so far."

"Really? Where have you been? You're still in county reds, so what are you doing in drug court?" I asked.

"Yeah well they have this gig at the Kent jail, this transitional program. It's in one of the units down there. You go to some out-patient classes and there's AA meetings a couple evenings a week, like outside guys come in and hold a meeting. It's about 60-90 days, then after that you can go to work release or housing and work on the rest of the program. Man there's a ton of people from the block in there right now, all from that bust. They can even get you on methadone before you get released so you have something to work with on the cravings. I'm not on it, but it's available. I just had a check in hearing here; now waiting for the transport back to Kent."

This information really caught me off guard. I've talked to a handful of people over the last few months about referrals to drug court, participation in the program, and all I've ever heard is how it's a "set-up". Nobody ever says how, but many of them just said it's a challenging program and difficult to complete. A lot of what I heard was that it was a year program, at minimum; could be two. Dizzy just told me a couple weeks back if he got of-fered drug court, he was going to say screw it, and take his case mainstream; eat the felony and time, and move on. He suggested I do the same.

"So what's your deal? Do you know what they're gonna do with you, after getting picked up on the bench warrant?" he asked.

"Fuck, to be honest? I really have no clue." I said.

"I'll tell you what man, if they give you the chance, take the TRP program. Don't think about it, just take it. They'll move you to Kent within a week or two, and we'll be able to catch up more there. If you don't like what happens, I think you can take your case mainstream at any time."

I don't remember even replying to Happy, I think I just sat there in silence. What in the hell kind of process would I be committing to? Is this seriously what they were trying to get me started on, 60-90 days in custody with treatment? Work release, housing after that, then what? The only other thing I heard about drug court is you only move forward towards graduation by staying clean. How does a guy like me do that? None of this made any sense.

But then again not a damn thing I was doing made any fucking sense either, to me or to anybody, for that matter. I was 32 years old, just establishing a criminal record, and looking at one to three years in prison. I had a no-contact order with my daughter's mother, hadn't seen my kid in over a month, and I had SPD and King County Sheriff's Department's attention. I was about to walk into drug court, with an assigned case manager I blew off by not showing up, a random attorney I've never met, some prosecutor to whom I'm likely just another offender on today's calendar, and the judge. And until they let me into the courtroom, the company I'm keeping is a room full of people who have spent months or years trying to do shit their way, getting their kinds of results, which in turn led them and me here. These are the current relationships in my life. And here's one thing I've learned about my addiction: I can't have regular, reasonable relationships with people like my family, partners, employers and my surrounding community when I'm using drugs and alcohol. Because in my experience, when I'm in my addiction, I serve that first and above everything else in my life.

"Conniff." I heard the door open, saw the guard, but actually forgot where I was for about five minutes. Then I suddenly felt like a game show contestant. There was this sense that if I could go out to that courtroom, say the right thing, maybe I could get out one more time, have one last good run, and somehow all of this other shit in my life would just go away. That would be the victory for today.

I looked over at Happy and gave him a brief nod, got up and got cuffed.

They walked me out to the courtroom and sat me in the jury box. I looked out over the regular benches and saw Brian. No shit? Man everybody is wrapped up in this drug court thing. Brian was one of the guys I would get my stuff from for a brief period of time. He was short, bald, and pretty funny for a guy running amuck out in the streets.

As Brian and I made eye contact, the attorney walked up to me in the box.

"Alright Mr. Conniff, here's the deal. You didn't show up to the orientation and haven't had any contact with the case manager. So the only offers look like TRP or mainstream. What's it gonna be?

"What's the deal with mainstream?" I asked.

"Well, you'll likely be released immediately, but you'll have to come back and go before a judge on the heroin delivery and cocaine possession charges, and it looks like you have an assault case in another court. It's hard to say how much but you'll do some time on the drug charges. Do you want a shot at getting clean? This is an opportunity, and the only time you can try for it. After you choose mainstream and get that ball rolling, you can't turn back."

"Ok, let's do TRP." I told her.

It just came out, and I couldn't believe it. I didn't hesitate, I didn't think about it at all. I potentially just signed myself up for at least another 90 days in jail; no clue how any of this works afterward and I could have walked out of this courthouse today.

She said, "Ok, when we get to the bench I'll tell them you'd like to participate in the TRP program, and since that's the recommendation, it'll likely be approved."

I got to the bench and they accepted my request to participate. I was probably in front of the judge all of three minutes. I was told that sometime very soon I would be transferred to the Maleng Regional Justice Center in Kent to begin the program. I couldn't help thinking of Happy sitting there, looking better than the Happy I spent a week in jail with in February. This thing was working for him so far. He was the only evidence I had that this drug court thing held any water.

That day in the courtroom, and with the advice from Happy was probably the first time in ten years that I had actually even taken advice, and made what would become a sound decision. By far the best decision of my life, to date. And to be honest, I wouldn't fully grasp the gravity of that choice for another six or seven months.

When I was brought back to the bullpen, Happy had already been moved. He seemed like a fucking ghost. The whole thing didn't even seem real right now. I started asking myself questions, like "why in the hell after all this time am I running into Happy?" and "why is he the one I'm running into if all those other guys from the bust are doing drug court?"

For those of you that have ever sat in a bullpen, or waited for a hearing that may be the decision of you remaining behind bars or not, you're aware that there are suddenly pockets of seemingly religious individuals behind bars at the moment before their hearing. Many of the inmates I've met have some form of prayer that may be overheard in hopes that "coming to God" when my ass is on fire, will ensure my release and good graces with the courts.

I felt that on this particular day, I didn't get a chance to say any prayers or rehearse my will and demands before my higher power (whatever the hell that was) in promise and return that I would learn to live differently and give up the dope, once and for all. Happy was the "god-shot", the person being put in my life, to serve a purpose, to carry a message; the first message that would have depth and weight, as the Big Book of AA says. He would be the first person in which I saw a program of recovery working that would fuel my desire for freedom from the bondage of drugs and alcohol.

Two days later I was reading a book in the pod when the call came from the guard desk, "Conniff-roll it up, you're going to the MRJC tonight."

8

Home Again

It didn't take long before I was back in full throttle on my cocaine addiction in Massachusetts. I returned home to my parent's place while I waited to pull the couple thousand dollars out of my retirement, and immediately Monica and I had gotten divorced. And just shortly before my return, my cousin Jack had gotten out of the Navy as well.

Once the check came from my retirement fund, my buddy Matt and I rented a place in Springfield. I managed to not put all of the money up my nose before getting the new apartment, but I sure did choose the right neighborhood for the next stage of my addiction to flourish.

The Forest Park and Belmont Heights section of Springfield probably had its good days back in the mid-20th century, but when I was home in 2005, the activity in the area around Euclid Ave and Belmont Ave was an addict's dream. Plus, being in Springfield put me closer to all my old connections and I quickly fell right back in with all the people I was hanging out with when I couldn't pass the piss test getting into the Navy.

I worked odd jobs for the first six months or so. One was doing flooring work for a friend of my old man's and the other was working with my sister's boyfriend building roof trusses. Both jobs ended the day with the work crews meeting up for cocktails, and by the time I made it home to Belmont Heights on most days, a gram of coke was the best idea I could come up with. Before long, Jack had begun renting an apartment at the Chestnut Towers, ten minutes up the road, and he was into much of the same post-work activities that I was. We got reckless in the evenings, and that tended to be on weeknights, compromising our abilities to remain employed.

Shortly after, another one of my cousins, Louie, returned home from the Navy as well. Louie, his sister, and my cousin Chris and his brother were all really close growing up and we regularly saw each other, especially around the holidays. Jack was from the other side of my family and didn't typically run in the same circles as Louie, but all of us were drinkers and users. To me, it felt really good to have cousins that served in the same branch, and now we were finally all home together.

The weekends were reserved for little gatherings at me and Matt's place, usually consuming ridiculous amounts of alcohol and me pooling money from a handful of folx to score blow. The thing about the people that came to party at our old Victorian rental was that they were all mostly disconnected from their families in terms of their behaviors and family dynamics. Many of them had come from households that lacked parental supervision or regular family routines. A good handful of them were younger kids from my old neighborhood across the river whose parents were alcoholics or they had different levels of dysfunction that happened in the home.

Even my friend Jeff from the skateboard days and I had started hanging out again. We kept talking about getting out on our boards, but every time I'd go to pick him up he'd have just scored some H and would nod off in the car on the way to the skate park. It seemed like everyone I knew was strung out on dope.

After prescription opiates rushed the legal drug market and finally became more costly and difficult to access, heroin addiction swept over my home town like a plague. Most of this transition occurred in those few years I was in the military. Even though I was well aware that Monica and a few of her close friends from high school had been consumed by dope, I really only ever saw that on the weekends when I would drive home. These other people coming to my place in the city would show up already strung out and nodding. It was hard to watch the people I spent my early years around now directionless and sucked up, so much that I didn't even see what was happening to me. I too was getting so fucking high on coke, I remember my parents being in the city occasionally on weekends and trying to stop by, and my having been up all night high as hell, I would peer out from the side of the curtains, ashamed to open the door. Hiding from my own family because I felt like a damn alien being whacked out while normal people got rest and did family things on the weekend.

For the next couple of months they kept trying to connect with me, and eventually I gave in a little bit.

My parents were making some moves to sell their house and move out to California to the warmer weather, and I started spending some time there after work helping my dad out touching up the house. He would offer to buy a few beers and have some dinner available, and besides needing a hand I think it was his attempt at trying to reel me away from my destructive lifestyle up in Springfield.

That worked for a short time, but before long I was working security at a bar and selling coke as my main sources of income, too busy and too high to spend quality time with my family.

Also, any time I came around my parent's house, I would wait for my mother to leave her room and I would run in and grab a handful of her Oxycodone 30's.

My mom was being prescribed over a 150 at a time and I had a dealer that would trade me $ .50/mg per pill for his coke. Occasionally I would keep one or two for myself to wind down, but at this time I never got hooked on opiates. What I've learned is that many people will attach themselves to substances that mimic their coping mechanisms, and for me at that time my coping was hypervigilance. After feeling like many of my relationships were out to screw me over, and being in countless problematic situations with Monica and the heroin game, I really held no interest in being dumbed down with opiates, so I remained dedicated to cocaine.

The next few months leading into the fall were disastrous. I barely stayed afloat with the dealers; and while working at the bar I got away with drinking. I always ended up using more when I drank, so I'd have to borrow money from my parents to make ends meet at the apartment. Finally, Matt and I had an unspoken falling out over the women coming to the house, as well as my drug activity, and I ended up back at my parent's place after all.

Worst part is they had sold the house and I only had about two months to try and pull my shit together.

My father never liked that I had moved up to the city, and my continuing drug use really only reinforced the idea that the inner city and people that lived there were the problem. It just didn't occur to find out why I used or what drugs did for me. He had the belief that if I just stayed away from people and places I would be better off.

My dad finally asked, "When the hell are you gonna have enough of this shit, Joe? When is it going to make sense that you have to stop? You can't hold a job, you lost the career in the Navy, and the only people you hang out with are strung out too."

I couldn't produce an answer. I wasn't upset with him, and it wasn't his fault for calling it as he saw it. Didn't he just want something better for me? Of course he did. Even I wanted to know why I couldn't just stop.

The way I felt about this only made matters worse. To the degree I was drinking now, even with Jack who was family, he and I would have disagreements when we hung out. I don't know what kind of turmoil he had going on internally and what drove him to his involvement with substances, but when we got together we usually just got stoned and watched the pile of drugs disappear before our eyes, leaving us bankrupt on many levels. After the come down and a day's rest we would get together and talk about the good days of the Navy and our aspirations over a meal, but inevitably trade all the dreamy thoughts in for some initial laughs over alcohol followed by a call to the coke dealer; alienating ourselves from the rest of the world to get lifted into a place that we just didn't have to feel.

I picked up a gig working at my buddy's pizza joint down by the river, but I mostly only ended up working to pay off last week's paycheck advances that went to drugs. I was fully enslaved. And the sense of getting the next bag of blow and half rack of beer was the only focus. If I could get lifted off just right I could forget, even for an hour, the painful experience of my inability to make it in life.

Since I had been back and got divorced, I also attempted to hold together a couple short relationships. For the most part it had only been drug fueled one nighters, but given my history with relationships, I became attached to any woman who responded intimately to me. I couldn't see past the old hurts and potential inevitable loneliness that came with my addiction and codependency.

I had those old damages, and I had medicated them for years now. So any act of personal vulnerability in a new setting gave way to extremely defeating, unwavering criticism of myself, and I would ultimately go on a runner destroying my chances of any positive relationship. Plus, I didn't understand unattached sex. Plain and simple. Relationships were just baffling to me, and by now at age 23-24, a lot of the people I grew up around or served with had been able to settle into some kind of healthy engagement with a partner. That just wasn't in the cards for me, at least at the rate I was going.

My parents finally packed up the house in early December of 2006, and my uncle and I drove a box truck of their belongings across the country. When I returned, I moved in with Denise and John; I had a room there and I continued on with the pizza shop.

After work I would isolate in my room to snort coke and drink alone.

At the same time an old acquaintance, Pete, got done serving some time. He was a bit older than me, and had quite a history of running drugs around our hometown. Since his release, he had been staying at my friend Will's house across town, and I started getting out more and kicking it with those guys. To date, after all the turbulent shit in my life, Will was the one grade school friend that I could always depend on. Even though he used as well, getting back in close contact with him felt like a refreshing experience. Our friendship was something more familiar from happier times in my life. Will and I went back so far and we never had a difference between us, not once in the 25 years I've known him.

Will came from a big family, mostly boys, and all of them were rough around the edges. They had a reputation around town as the kind of guys you didn't fuck with, because if you got into it with one of them, there were likely a couple more of them close by, and they all could and would throw down.

Shortly before my parents moved away, my sister had stopped using coke. Once she had caught onto me doing it in her house, her support of me staying there dwindled quickly. So after a couple of on and off weeks with Will and Pete, I started staying over there regularly, and eventually brought over whatever I could fit in my Navy sea bag. Will's girlfriend was pregnant and they were gradually moving out, so his younger brother Brad and I basically took up residence with Pete.

Pete was moving a lot of blow, and some heroin on the side. He had developed business relations from his time behind bars with people in New York, Hartford and upper Vermont, by the

Canadian border. He was well capable of moving weight week over week and it required regular trips to and from the other cities, downloading to a few of us to push eight balls and quarter ounces around the town bar scenes, and the rest went up north to his guy we called Uncle Rick in Vermont.

Pete was the kind of guy that didn't flaunt being a dope dealer in the clothes he wore or cars he drove. He kept it basic with t-shirts, jeans and plain sedans. He was the youngest of his siblings and had managed to stow away some cash before going away that was able to help the family out financially while he was inside, and that remained his biggest concern, far above his own wellbeing. In many of our conversations he was convinced he wouldn't amount to much past doing time and selling drugs, yet he believed in the abilities of his friends and taking care of his family members.

Say what you want about drug dealers, but hell, everyone has some sort of values, even the most unskillful people in the world care about something or someone. I'm sure there are people who'll read this and say "nope, he sold drugs, he's a dirt bag." And I get it. Yet I also knew the person beneath the behaviors, and Pete was capable of great things. I spent day in and day out with this guy for some time and he genuinely cared about the people in his life, and he supported them however possible.

"Joey, you can do this stuff with me for a while, and that's cool. But I don't want you thinking this is the last stop. You don't need to do this forever, you're gonna do better things. You don't want to be around someone like me much longer." he used to say to me. And this wasn't stuff he said loaded, this was him over breakfast before we would do a drive to Vermont.

There were a few occasions where he asked me to be the wheel man for the Vermont runs, given he wasn't supposed to cross state lines after his release; to top it off he was usually bringing a few hundred grams of dope with us to deliver. He was as strict as one could be about running dope too. No partying the night before the run; we'd get up and eat a full breakfast, minimum pit stops along the way, and no use on the trip either. Once we got to Vermont, Uncle Rick would meet us somewhere, have us hole up wherever he was staying, and he would run his deliveries for the night, usually returning early the next morning with profit and re-up money. Once we'd get back to Massachusetts, Pete and I would sit down and count everything from the week, usually tens of thousands of dollars, and meet up with the rest of our crew and party up for a couple days until it was time to work a run again.

During these couple of months, he and I became really close. We spent damn near all of our time together and focused on running his little dope business. As of April, we had been doing a lot of activity in the neighborhood and Pete was looking to move into another place in Springfield. He had some household items and furniture in storage up in Maine and we were planning to take the ride up there to get some of the housewares to set up the apartment he had put the deposit down on.

Tuesday evening was a typical night, doing some deliveries with Pete around town to our friends in the bars. He wasn't into personally selling small amounts, so he would hand off five to seven grams to one of his other guys and let them sell it off before they could call for a re-up. Around 8 p.m. my cousin called and wanted a little package on the other side of town to start celebrating his birthday. Pete agreed we could do one last stop to see him before calling it a night and turning in to get rested for the trip to Maine the following morning.

When we got back to the house, Pete had his heroin connection swing some product through, hang out for a few, and he and Pete snorted a few lines of the H. Pete was known to smoke some of it on foil from time to time so it wasn't exactly out of the ordinary for him to use some. I hit the couch as usual and crashed for the night. Our buddy, Gavin, was staying over to help out with the Maine trip as well.

Sometime before 8 a.m. I overheard Gavin saying Pete's name, and then he rushed into the living room.

"Joe man we're late and Pete won't wake up. I think something's going on with him."

"What do you mean?" I asked as I got up and headed towards Pete's room. When I opened the door, Pete was laying on his back, and he was snoring in a really strange tone with a disturbing gurgling sound.

"Pete. Hey Pete!" I started trying to shake his shoulder a bit, Gavin was pacing all around the room. "What the fuck do you think is happening man?" he asked me.

"I don't know man, get me my fucking phone! Pete! Pete! Come on man, get up!" I kept calling out to him as Gavin came in with my phone.

"What are you doing?" he asked.

I said, "I'm calling 911."

"Are you fucking serious? There's a bunch of dope, scales, a gun, money. You're fucking kidding right?" he was dumbfounded.

"Let me get someone on their way and I'll figure it out, I have the second key to the safe, and Pete's is on the nightstand."

I called 911, gave them the address and let them know my friend wouldn't wake up"and had erratic breathing. I got off the phone and went back to trying to get some response out of Pete, but nothing.

Pete had a safe that he had mounted into the floor of the closet with seven inch lag bolts, and it held all the dope and cash. Plus, he had a tactical fold-out stock shotgun under the bed. The safe required two keys to open, so I threw Gavin the duffel bag next to the bed and opened the safe so he could get the gun and dope out of the house.

"What do I do?" he asked.

"Take this shit out the door and go to Mike's house up the street. Tell him what's happening. I'll stay with Pete."

Gavin flew down the stairs out of the house, and I ran back into the room and continued calling Pete's name, shaking him, trying to turn him onto his side. I had no idea what was happening, and for all I knew he was choking. That didn't help, so I turned him back over to his back. I had some first responder training from the Navy so I started in on chest compressions and mouth to mouth, back and forth for a couple of rounds.

Then I heard the sirens coming from Springfield Street, but there were already other footsteps coming up the backstairs.

I looked out the window and there was an unmarked police car blocking the driveway, and the ambulance was just turning onto the street. Just then the police walked into the house.

"Sir, you need to come over here and sit down at the table." said the first cop in plain clothes.

"Hurry up, he's over here in this room." I said.

"Hey, I'm not going to ask again. Sit down at the table before I cuff you to the chair."

"What the fuck?" I asked, "He's in that room and he's....." suddenly I was pulled from behind and forced into the chair.

"We know who Pete is; we've been watching you guys and know what you've been up to for a little while now." the other one said. The first cop was now moving through the house, rifling through the cabinets and trash barrel.

"Look man, are you gonna fucking do something to help him?" I asked.

Right then, the officer standing behind me cuffed me to the chair.

As the other cop was pulling cut baggies from the trash and placed another scale on the table that I missed packing up with Gavin, the paramedics came through the door.

There was a solid five minutes that I was in that house with the two undercovers that the paramedics were in front of the house but had not come up the stairs yet. All of it felt like a set up, and Pete was in there in bad shape.

And then finally in walked a uniformed cop. I knew him from the days when he was a D.A.R.E. officer in the school system.

"Joe, is that Pete in there?" he asked.

By now the medics had come in and I could hear them trying to get his attention, and they counted to three as they lifted him onto the stretcher.

"Yeah it is. What are these other guys doing? They were in here before the paramedics and they didn't even go into the fucking room? They're going through all kinds of shit in the house."

He got me uncuffed from the chair and took me into the other room.

"Look Joe, they have a good idea of what you've all been up to."

"Yeah, what's that?"

"Are you serious?" he asked.

"Ok, and is that an excuse to not give someone fucking medical attention?"

"What did Pete do? Do you know what's wrong with him?"

"Man if I knew do you think I would have called 911, the fuck if I know?! He was snorting some dope last night, last time I spoke to him was at 11 p.m. I just woke up at eight and he wasn't breathing right."

"Was anybody else here last night, like anybody else stay over?" he asked.

"Nope. Just me and Pete."

"Hey, you gotta see this." one of the plain clothes had piped up, "There's a safe in here, bolted to the floor."

Little did they know, after I sent Gavin out, I left Pete's key in the safe door and threw mine out the bedroom window, figuring regardless of the outcome the safe was going to be of interest. The only thing left in there were spare buttons that went to Pete's nice dress shirts and some cheap jewelry.

"What's in the safe kid?" he asked.

"Your guess is as good as mine."

Right then, the medics were getting ready to take Pete feet first down the stairs on the stretcher. Those gurgling noises (which I now know is referred to in overdoses as the "death rattle") had stopped, and I didn't hear any more of the erratic breathing. The medics were silent as they took him out of the house.

It dawned on me in that moment that he died right there in that fucking room; and I felt inadequate in my ability to save him, or get him the help he needed. That morning Pete would become a casualty of the war on drugs; due to stigma and poor policy enforced by biased police.

Opiate overdoses weren't as easily reversed by the general population in 2007 as they are nowadays, solely because Narcan wasn't something that non-medic folx carried around or had ready access to in comparison to now, likely due to the fact that we weren't quite in the heart of the opioid epidemic and how to be prepared to respond to it.

It's extremely challenging for me to detail all of the events of that morning, March 7, 2007. Deaths like Pete's and hundreds of thousands of others would eventually lead us to a place that would implore friends and family members to be ready at any time for the overdose of a loved one. I can't help but think about what would have been different about that morning had I known, had policy about drugs and addiction led us down a path of compassion and understanding rather than stigma and continuous criminalizing responses. After all, he was still a drug user; not just a dealer.

After Pete was out of the house, and the closet safe was discovered, the interest in me was worn out. The old D.A.R.E. officer walked out with Pete's body, and I recall somewhere in the conversation that occurred while I was cuffed to the chair that he mentioned growing up and going to school with Pete's older brother, so I think he felt an obligation to see off the final moments. The other two plain clothes asked for my info, uncuffed me and continued to toss the house. I walked on out after the ambulance left and headed up to Mike's house to catch up with him and Gavin. How do I tell them what just happened?

The way that I felt on that three block walk is indescribable. By now I had put everything together that it was an overdose, but that didn't make things feel anymore settled, nor did it relieve me of the guilt I felt for not being able to help him in those seven to ten minutes since I woke up and the cops and medics arrived. So much had happened so fast. If I could do it over, what could I have done differently? Would anything have changed the outcome? Would he still be here today?

We jumped in my car parked outside of Mike's, since I let him use it when I did trips with Pete, and we headed to the hospital. Gavin and Mike asked me what I thought was happening and I didn't have the fucking courage to tell them what I was quite sure what I knew to be true; that he was already gone.

After twenty minutes in the waiting room, ten of those minutes with Pete's older sister, a doctor came to talk to us. He didn't make it. But I already knew this, yet receiving confirmation and watching everyone else's reaction made me sick to my fucking stomach. People loved Pete. I was the last one with him, and I felt compelled and responsible over the next ten days to explain what our last hours together had been like.

We had a funeral service and celebration of life for Pete on St. Patrick's Day over by the lakes. Mike, Gavin and I spent the week and a half leading up to it tying up Pete's loose business ends and selling off the dope that was in the safe that morning. We were able to come back with a little over $7,000 dollars, all of it went to his sister to pay for the funeral and support the get together for family and friends after the services.

Within two weeks after Pete's funeral I was on a plane to Denver. I had called my old Navy buddy Tommy and he said he could get me a job driving a delivery truck; I could stay with him for a while, so off I went. I couldn't handle Massachusetts anymore; I fucking despised everything about my life there, especially in the last few months. I lost my good friend; my parents had moved away; my relationship with my sister was strained and I was completely distraught and broken. I woke up with anxiety every day, reliving the events of that morning in March, wanting so badly to escape and get loaded. But the truth was that I was unemployable, broke, and pretty much homeless in my car except for the few nights a week I stayed at Westfield State College (now Westfield State University) on my friend's dorm couch.

Denver brought the hopes of a geographical change to save me. I got set up with a job driving and delivering mattresses all over Colorado, and I made good money. I was making about $700-$800 per week and Tommy only charged me $500 a month for rent.

Chuck, another friend from the Navy was living out there, and since he had a vehicle and I had good income, we spent a lot of time hiking, playing golf, and I got heavy back into billiards. The only problem with the money I was making is that I was drinking like it was my second job after parking the work truck. I always made rent and phone bills, but honestly at $550 a month in bills, and $3000 a month in income, I spent most days after work at the bar with the other alcoholics. Scooters was the lounge about a fifteen minute walk from my place with Tommy, and I went straight there after work. On most of my days off I was there from open until closing. Degenerative alcoholism, at its worst. But hey, at least I went to work every day and paid my bills, that was my logic. There was no growth, no movement towards self-betterment, and no intention to achieve a bigger purpose; let alone heal from the trauma of Pete's death.

One month into my work we were driving into Central City, Colorado when I got a call from my cousin, Chris. I hadn't really spoken to him much since I left Massachusetts so I was eager to catch up.

"What's up?"

"Not a whole hell of a lot. Got some bad news Joe." he said.

"Yeah, what's that? I asked.

"Jeff was found dead, he OD'd in his car on break at work."

At that moment, I just sat quiet, processing what my cousin told me. I wasn't prepared to hear this now, and told Chris I had to get off the phone; that I'd call him back.

One month before I left I had heard Jeff was doing better, but apparently it didn't stick. Hearing this was too difficult. Two close friends down in four and a half months, both to heroin. I don't think that news changed my drinking habits all that much, given nothing had changed significantly around my alcohol intake since Pete's passing. Not that it wasn't a problem, but I don't think it could have gotten noticeably worse.

Soon enough, I began looking for some comfort in women again. It started with the secretary at work, who put up with my drinking for reasons beyond me. She was lovely, too. Super compassionate, caring and generous; and I was just looking for companionship with no ability to get into the meat of a relationship. Shelly was tall, dark long brown hair and laid back. Unfortunately for her, my emotions were empty, and all I wanted was physical connection. I barely had the capacity to appreciate her just for existing, let alone spending time with me. She was consistently kind and there for me; but how the fuck can you love or appreciate someone else when you can't do that for yourself?

Then there was another woman, Gina, that I met through a drinking buddy, and she was from Colorado Springs. She was Italian, had two kids, and with that came the thought that this would be a solution to all of my problems; the family thing. Man did I want to make that one work; she was outgoing, fun and responsible as an adult.

What in the hell did I think I was offering besides an evening of drinks? Outside of alcohol I didn't hold much charisma. My appreciation of the arts and entertainment was still that of Reservoir Dogs, gangster movies and comedians like Dane Cook. Nothing wrong with enjoying those things, but that's the shit I talked about in my spare time. Sure, grown women are really into my ability to quote Christopher Walken movies and drink a bottle of Sambuca. Then again I was about 24 years old, relatively young; yet with no college experience and an Other Than Honorable (OTH) discharge from the Navy, it was easy to see I wasn't on track for great things. I didn't discuss aspirations, probably because I didn't have any, and because I knew it was just a matter of time before the drug use would return.

And that it did. Eventually the Colorado Springs relationship became strained due to the long distance and my behaviors, I imagine, and eventually she broke things off.

I had been relatively removed from my regular haunts since starting that relationship, and more often than not I would just drink at home, but nevertheless, I was drinking a lot. After the split, I started hitting the bar scene again regularly. The guy I met Gina through had a new friend around that could get coke. This was great news to me.

Within two months, I was dating a bartender at Scooters and we were taking coke orders for the bar patrons and getting a bunch for free. I literally quit the truck driving gig almost overnight once I met Tina, primarily because I was too busy selling coke and staying out all night partying. When she went to work at the bar, I went in with her, and would spend most of the evening blowing lines off of the backs of toilets and driving to the dealer's house to pick up orders.

Drug fueled relationships can only go so far for so long, and eventually we were really no longer in a romantic relationship. The bar manager was onto my dealing, suspected her involvement, and since she had a ten year old boy being raised by her mother that she was trying to get back, she couldn't have her livelihood compromised, and I moved in with Chuck briefly.

Chuck's younger brother Danny was spending some time with us, having made the drive from Wyoming to catch up with his brother, and he was an on the fly "fuck it, let's do it" kind of guy. He talked me into moving up to Wyoming with him until we pooled together enough cash to go on a West Coast road trip for the summer.

In almost no time the summer was upon us, neither of us were yet employed, and the ability to fund a two month road trip was non-existent.

"Do you know where we can get any dope?" he asked me one day.

"Like what?" I asked.

"Crystal, coke, anything really. I've got a little money put aside, if we can get some stuff in Denver for a decent price we can take it back up to Wyoming and flip it for a great profit. Maybe we can get a place and some jobs up there if we fall back on the dope for a month or so."

"Sure can." I told him.

I had just the guy, the old connection from the bar. Funny thing was he had just been calling with a nice price, and if I had some cash, he could really put me on.

Over the next month and half, I did about five or six trips back and forth from Denver to Newcastle, Wyoming in supplying my habit and the habit of the 20's something individuals around Weston County. I had never really been around the methamphetamine scene, but was now supplying it. We spent the first couple weeks camping out in the Black Hills, then crashing on couches surrounded by tweakers at it for two to three days at a time. We had guys that worked on the oil derricks picking up the coke and meth, bringing it out to the job sites and turning it around awfully fast, which was good but hard to keep up with. During this time, Danny went back to legitimate work, and I began doing the Denver run with another guy.

I needed to find real employment before my presence along with the influx of dope in an extremely small town led to questions about the little circle we had going. I started applying for bartending gigs and eventually landed one two doors down from the place we began renting. It was an old flour mill, with a bar/

lounge and a drive through liquor store below, and cafe/restaurant on the other side. The business had been up and running for a good thirty years, but was recently sold to a group of three owners. The bar needed a manager and full time employee, so I took on the task of both since it would suffice financially and get me out of the dope running.

Honestly I really needed to slow things down after those first couple months in the Black Hills. I had been running hard the last months in Denver and being spun out around these folx while trying to settle in had really taken its toll on my mental health. Not that it wasn't already compromised by my use, but I had really only been getting 15-20 hours of sleep per week and eating like shit for the last five months.

The first couple weeks at the bar I really took things seriously. I had something that needed my attention, and I dug in. I did one more Denver trip after getting started and gave up on the drug running for a little while. Working at the bar for 12-15 hour shifts around casual drinkers and alcoholics had me diving head first back into my daily drinking though.

Here's the thing about Newcastle. The majority of the employment available is at the oil refinery, coal mine, or out on the derricks in Gillette. A lot of these positions were swing shifts, or four on three offs, and a good portion of the town's population would be intoxicated by 11 a.m. at the local bars and pubs, and it was perfectly acceptable and a local norm to do so.

The Sturgis bike rally was less than two hours away and leading up to August the town drew a lot of motorcycle traffic. I managed to really get the bar business off the ground around that time and with it went my drinking. I drank about a fifth or more of Jack Daniel's everyday along with a good twelve pack of beer, and anything the customers asked me to drink in between.

You could think one would be extremely overwhelmed by growing up in New England, spending time in cities like Denver or Norfolk, and then landing in Wyoming; but given the nature of my drinking, the bar, and abundance of alcoholism present it gave me a sense of fitting in again, no matter how small of a town it was.

Preparing for the amount of traffic the business would see for the Sturgis rally, one of the bosses flew his two daughters out to help out with the restaurant and train the staff. Both of the women had plenty of experience in the service industry, and they flew in from Seattle for about a week and a half stay.

I met Rachael the day she got there as her father was showing her around the lounge. At first we didn't interact much given how the overall business was, but by the third night of closing down together we caught up over a few drinks in the bar.

We went on hanging out over the next week, and by the time she left, we had a little thing going. I stayed on working for her Dad, but we had also gotten a couple part time employees which allowed for me to take a trip up to Seattle to visit and get to know her mom and other family in the Pacific Northwest. Rachael was a heavy marijuana user; and the fact that she was engaged in some kind of use allowed me to falsely convey the true nature of my drinking in hopes that I could stay on with my alcoholism so long as she was still getting high.

As far as the visit to Seattle, part of me was really excited. This presented itself as another end all for the insanity of life on my own. Rachael and I discussed my moving up to Seattle for good, and I knew my drinking was unmanageable in Wyoming. Things were getting questionable in relation to my performance at the bar as well. I hung out there extremely intoxicated on my days off, and basically woke up every morning physically sick from my body's dependence on booze, so there was no way I was going to be able to operate this way in Seattle. I couldn't even get out of bed without a glass of Jack Daniel's to stop the shaking and dry heaving. These weren't hangovers either, this was late-stage alcoholism. The closer I neared going to Seattle, the more I began to self-sabotage accessing what I thought I wanted so badly; a relationship. I even disengaged from Rachael all together and entered into a runner that I have no idea when it started or ended. I remember not wanting to wake up; I thought I could kill myself drinking, and was awfully close to being successful at it.

My friend came over one morning and saw the whiskey bottles all around my bed and said, "What are you doing man? You're a good guy Joe, don't do this to yourself. You deserve better. Get it together for a few days and get the hell out of here. This place will kill a guy like you."

What kind of guy am I, really? I was asking myself. I knew that I had much internal work to do to be in a real relationship, to build a future, and I had so many poor beliefs about my emotional intelligence. I was well aware that I had never processed that day losing Pete, let alone anything else in my life prior. For the most part I was delusional about my relationship to drugs and alcohol, as I firmly believed they were helping get me through my tough times, unaware that they were slowly dismantling the road ahead.

9

Pacific Northwest

Finally the day came when I was to get a ride to the nearest airport, Rapid City, South Dakota, to move to Seattle. Moving for me meant packing my sea bag with a pool cue and clothes, which could all be done in five to ten minutes. For a good seven years, everything I had to my name fit into that bag, because material possessions weren't of much interest to me. My focus was always on the next drink or drug, as it was the day of the flight.

I got to the Bronco Bar at 11 a.m. and had a 3 p.m. flight. Rapid City was a little over an hour away, so I thought I'd have a few drinks before heading to the airport. By 11:30 a.m. the bar turned into a going away party. My ride came to get me, though I don't remember the drive, and by 2:30 p.m. when I was prepared to board, I was so hammered I wasn't allowed on the flight. Danny came to get me, and I had to make the phone call to Rachael about how I would have to wait until tomorrow to try again.

By the time I got to Seattle the following afternoon, Rachael had enough of my drinking, but seeing as I was going to be physically sick from withdrawal, I spent a few days easing down on beer only. I actually remained abstinent for a period of a few months, and during that time we went to visit my parents in California as my relationship with Rachael grew more serious.

I landed a job as a produce wholesaler, spending time each week out of town in Eastern Washington, and I got to the point of hashing out plans to start a small food production business with an entrepreneurial friend. For the most part, things were going really well. But after a few months, Rachael and I had a ferocious argument and I went down to take a break from the relationship at my parent's place in California. Surprisingly, the fight had nothing to do with my drinking, but of course I would go on to medicate the loss of the relationship with alcohol once I got to SoCal.

Things with my mom and dad weren't going so well health-wise, but while I was there I helped them out a lot around the house and with doctor's appointments during the daytime. My mother was now primarily onto marijuana, with the booming medical-grade movement around 2009. My dad had a lot of vision problems and required a wheelman for most of his doctor appointments.

At night though, I began frequenting bars around town, playing pool for side money, finally landing a few days a week working at a biker bar. Outside of bartending, I really didn't keep any other company. By now I sure knew where to find my sub-culture for survival when I got disconnected from purpose and any possibility of healing.

While I was there my cousin Jack reached out to me, and he sounded good. Towards the last days in Massachusetts I had heard he was in the county jail for a charge or two. We talked on the phone for a bit one afternoon, and he wanted to pull me in on a trip he was preparing to take.

"Hey man I'm headed to Peru, taking a journey and some time off from here. Going to check out Machu Picchu, all of that!" he said.

"When are you going?" I asked.

"In the end of May. You should come along!" he exclaimed.

"Shit man, I'm here helping my parents out, and don't exactly have the cash for that kind of thing. Sounds awesome for sure though!"

"Well let's get together when I get back; I'll come down and visit. It'd be great to see your folks anyways." he said.

"For sure, stay safe and I'll look forward to hearing from you!" I said.

Damn. He sounded good, and he was happy. Actually excited about something on the horizon, and he was able to plan out for that sort of thing, which to me seemed baffling. I couldn't seem to get past working week to week and planning for a day trip to San Clemente on the weekend.

The break to Cali didn't last more than four months before Rachael and I smoothed stuff out and I went back to Seattle.

When I returned, I got a job selling fasteners and industrial supplies in south Seattle and was doing fairly well with that. It wasn't my favorite position, but it definitely helped pay the bills. For the most part things in our relationship seemed fairly steady, though we had drinks at night, and there was still consistent pot smoking.

Finally I discovered that Rachael's brother liked to do coke, so when she and I would get into any type of argument, I'd end up over there doing lines and drinking with him for a night, but there definitely weren't big, two to three day long runners yet. Making it to work and getting along held priority. Plus we had recently moved into a less expensive apartment in Queen Anne; it was close to work and still a fun neighborhood at the time.

In early June 2010, I was at work and missed a call from my cousin, Chris. He left a message and said it was about Jack and that I should call him back.

"Hey man, what's happenin?" I asked.

"You got a minute Joe?"

"Yeah, what's up?"

Chris said, "Jack's dead; he was murdered down in Peru."

"What the fuck?"

"Yeah, we don't really know anything else or have details. Something happened at the place he was staying. We just found out, but you should come back for the services once we know more. Can you make it?" he asked.

"Yeah, definitely."

He said, "Ok, I'll keep you posted. His body still needs to be returned to the states. Might be a couple weeks."

I hung up and just fucking lost it. I just saw his post on Facebook two days before about him getting there and pics of one of the first hiking excursions he had gone on. He had invited me on this trip.

Not even five minutes later my parents called and reported the same news. No other details either.

After a massive fiasco between Jack's family and the authorities in Peru, his body was finally on the way home. I was tight on money as usual and had to borrow money from an aunt and uncle to make the trip, adding to the guilt and shame I carried from my falling outs with family over my drug use.

I spent the time in between his death and the trip home drinking heavily from the minute I got off work until the minute I passed out, leading to arguments and unease at home.

When I finally got back to Massachusetts, it had been three years since I left; and I had taken off on the heels of Pete's death which was a chaotic time for me and communications with family members. I never said goodbyes since I had been so fucked up and closed off from them for those two years after my discharge from the Navy.

Naturally, around Jack's tragic passing, there was a lot of drinking going on from the day I showed up. Of course my drinking led a few family members to believe that I was using coke again the first two days I was home. I wasn't, and I don't blame anyone for not believing me. I hadn't yet acted in a way that would have provoked other expectations of me during this visit.

After the burial and enough drinking and accusations from family about potential drug use, I stormed off to my sister Denise's and was offered to stay there for the rest of the trip. Will heard I was back in town and wanted to catch up, so he scooped me and I spent a few days with him and the old crew from the days with Pete. Will had experienced significant loss of an ex and three of his closest friends in his late teens, and he was helpful and compassionate in being there for me with the loss of Jack. Of course I used coke being back in that company, a rekindling of my old patterns of coping behaviors.

The next night we went out to the bar and I felt awful. It was the first time I had been home since Pete's death and now I was lit as hell in the same bar where he and I were the last night he was alive. When we went back to Will's house in the early hours of the morning, and I remember I couldn't stop crying about the tragedies that befell the people I knew and loved. I never learned to deal with the loss of Pete, and by now Jack was buried and I was trying to fuck myself up to oblivion with this loss too; no progress in working with my emotions, just disbelief and self-destruction.

Most of all, it was difficult to see my family and friends on this trip. Many of them had started families of their own, had careers, and were raising kids. I had drifted along since my discharge and hadn't strung together much of anything. I left there feeling motivated to try and settle down into a life in Washington, but only by comparing myself to others and where I felt I should have been by this point in my life.

I returned to Seattle, focused on trying to start a family, and we were pregnant by July expecting a daughter in late March of 2011.

The road of the pregnancy was absolute hell for Rachael and I'm quite sure because I made it a fucking nightmare. I made her suffer through my ongoing alcoholism and addiction, unaddressed grief and traumas during all of it, never acknowledging the gravity of the pregnancy and starting a family. I couldn't even take care of myself; how was I going to provide stability and a future for her and a child?

Two months after Jack's funeral and early into the pregnancy I had left the fastener sales job and went to work again as a produce wholesaler for a large farm in Eastern Washington. Before long I found out that many of the employees used cocaine and I was relieved to know that when things got uncomfortable at home I could always hang with them and escape my reality. More times than not, the impending birth and expectations of fatherhood scared the hell out of me, and I regularly started arguments at home to go use.

I was the worst partner. I took the car and money on payday, oftentimes not returning when I said I would, and usually a couple of hundred dollars short. Both of us worked for the farm, so she knew roughly what the pay should have been, and since the work was off the books, it was easy for me to spend out of it right away on a Sunday night by seeing the dealer twenty minutes after meeting the boss for payroll.

The turmoil at home due to my using and stress I put on my relationship was unreal. I have no doubt that it had its adverse effects not just on her but on my unborn child. I didn't understand planning for a family; I didn't help schedule doctor's appointments. I was just plain unreliable and unavailable in all aspects of life.

Right around November of 2010 when the harvest season slowed, our financial difficulties increased and I sought relief and freedom the only way a selfish addict/alcoholic knows how; so after another one of the arguments, I left and went down to California again on my parents dime. I knew I could tell them anything I pleased about what transpired with Rachael, and they'd believe whatever, and I could continue to medicate my emotions the way I saw fit. I knew the environment at my folk's place; I knew the way my mother medicated, and I knew that was a safe place for me and my thinking.

Back in Cali in a matter of just three months before the birth, I had managed to get another job at a bar, started as a hang-around and became a prospect with a local 1% motorcycle club after becoming good friends with one of their enforcers. I also established a coke connect there in town. Of course my access to drugs and use of them established my legitimacy and security with the club. I had a perfect brilliance for finding people that accepted my way of living and dealing with life.

The status with the club wasn't exactly something I asked for, but I wasn't going to turn it down. I felt like I needed it for survival at this point in my life. It was an identity, and people wanted me to be part of it. It was the first time in a while that anybody actually asked me to be part of something. Many of them were veterans, some had completed their service honorably discharged, and others were misfits like myself. Some were Marines from Twenty-Nine Palms, and others were from other branches and states. Either way, there was brotherhood and comradery again. There were fights, drugs, guns and women, all in abundance, all at the same time.

I actually made the trip to Seattle around the time my daughter was to be born, and once I was back, I felt cornered and compromised. I was surrounded by Rachael's family and I felt vulnerable without my support system from the club. The night before she went into labor, I went for a drink, had more than one, came back and argued with her father for a bit, and then took off drinking for the rest of the night. There was no reason for my drinking other than I couldn't handle hearing what her family thought of me; which is what I believed was actually true of me; that I was selfish and irresponsible.

Somewhere in the events of that evening that I don't recall, I purchased a plane ticket by phone, and got on a flight the next morning. I went on to miss the birth of my daughter because I couldn't accept my realities; the reality of the damage I caused in my use and the reality of becoming a father. In my mind, this will always remain as the most disgraceful thing I did in my addiction. It's never about the drugs that we use or how we use them, whether you shoot, snort or smoke. It's about what I sacrifice and who else suffers when I'm using that makes me an addict. I'm already in pain, that's why I use; but the fact that my being in pain and how I choose to medicate it causes suffering in the life of others, is a larger issue that only perpetuates my insatiable craving. Not being there for the birth of my daughter due to substance use ought to have sealed the deal that I and my priorities were fucked up. But when I landed in Palm Springs, I stayed on drinking and getting high with the club for the next forty-eight hours.

Once I finally came down and found out that Ione Swan was born on April 2, 2011, I remained on the fence both about my desire to be in the club and my desire to be a Dad. For many, this may seem absolutely pathetic and ridiculous to have to discern what one should do in this situation, but to me, it meant to leave behind something familiar, that provided my kind of comforts, for something that was totally foreign and required growth, humility and love. All three were things I believed I was incapable of.

I did finally come to enough sense that I needed to be there for my daughter, so I got another plane ticket, left the familiarity of the fast life behind, and flew back to Seattle for good. The next farm season was on the horizon and I figured I could stay with the guys, make some money to support my daughter and start building a future.

Ione was close to two months old when I finally met her. Her mother picked me up at the airport and I broke down the minute I laid eyes on the innocent, beautiful little human looking back at me. We took her to the Olympic Sculpture Park in Seattle on a cloudy afternoon and I held her for the first time, and couldn't believe how incredible I felt. I had been trading this opportunity for drugs and alcohol for the last two months, and the entire pregnancy leading up to it.

As unfortunate as the events at home in my childhood were, and the lack of attention to my emotional needs, it still wouldn't have occurred to my parents to not be there for me, at least in physical form. It's really fucking terrible that I couldn't understand that so long as I had relationships with drugs and alcohol, I wouldn't be able to be a father to my daughter. I wouldn't be able to nurture that relationship that she needed, and that I needed as well. I just couldn't have one foot in fatherhood and a whole leg in my addiction. My experience shows me that I'll get pulled under by dope, and the people in my life will always suffer.

I jumped right back into working the markets and wholesaling on the road a few days a week, which put me back into that place of feeling lonely and alone with my thoughts, three hours at a time from Yakima to Seattle. With that came the craving for cocaine, that familiar state of hypervigilance. I would score some in Yakima and white-knuckle the ride back to Seattle high as a fucking kite on what would become two to three hours of sleep on the nights I went back and forth from the farm.

I got to see Ione about two to three days a week, depending on my drive days, and most weekends. In what seemed like a matter of weeks, it was the end of the harvest season again, and my having a spot with the guys was gone until they came back to rent seasonally the following spring.

The off seasons were when things got really tricky for me. The finances would always thin out in November and I'd get stuck taking some kind of food service work to help support my daughter and her mother. We ended up moving back in with Rachael's mother for a bit, but given the fact that I left before the birth, that relationship was strained on my end, as it should have been. That lasted through an off season and once we were back up and running with the farm again, we managed to get a nice two bedroom in Burien, between Seattle and Tacoma, which worked out well for most of the sales work.

During the time with the farm operations I got connected to a coke dealer in Queen Anne, and I was stopping by to meet him regularly during my delivery shifts. I often had cash on hand, and the dealer needed a lift here and there so I would get little hookups just for driving. By the arrival of another off season, I was really feeling the pull of my heightened rewards and relief system that was not getting met by my usual stops through the Queen Anne neighborhood, and the routine hits of coke throughout my day. It had become such a part of my work and life schedule that to not do it felt like part of me was missing, almost dying.

I inevitably created an argument and a need to go out one evening, and it landed me on a bender where I left the car parked with the key stashed in the wheel well, and sent a text to my daughter's mother of the whereabouts of the car. And that was that. I turned my cell phone off and never turned it back on until this go around ended. That runner lasted three months.

During that time I holed up with the coke dealer, whose business partner was recently hospitalized, and he utilized me to keep operations going in the trap house on the first floor of the building. On an average day we would turn about fifty to sixty grams of blow, and most of the time the folx that bought the stuff would just stay there and use it. Along with a place to stay, I had 24/7 access to drugs. I slept from 6 a.m. to noon, and we were basically open for business at all other hours of the day.

This was almost the perfect fix. For those of us that have tried to stay high forever, this was probably the closest I had ever gotten to achieving that. In no other time in the history of my addiction was I able to maintain a constant high, so much that from the minute I woke up I had access to use until the minute I crashed out. After such a long day of being strung out and the constant flow of alcohol, my body found it rather easy to call it quits once the early morning hours arrived. All I had to do was keep serving the customers, and my guy would supply the goods to keep me tight.

Of course I thought about my daughter in all of this, but what did I have to offer? That was the question I asked myself. Even now it hurts like hell to think about the periods of her life that I wrote the fuck off because of my use. I wanted to be there for her, I really did. I wanted to play at the park with her, I wanted to take walks with her. I wanted to hold her and tell her I loved her, but as always, I didn't love myself. I stayed on this runner just to try and float above the dissatisfaction with myself.

This place was crazy. It was right across the street from Key Arena, and the characters that came through there were something else altogether. I heard so many stories of just straight broken homes and horrible childhoods. There were well to do software guys that came through and spent $400-$500 on coke for the weekend parties on their boats, and then there were other people like me, just looking for a temporary flight from whatever unsettled them. Really we were all just a bunch of lost souls that thought we had found a common remedy to the challenges of our worlds. And when we were in our use, we all found the same sense of freedom, and we were all welcome at the trap house.

The building in itself was its own special type of milieu. The boss lived upstairs, and helped pay the rent for the guy downstairs (whose place I stayed in while he was hospitalized) because of the coke running through his doors. But there were two to three other tenants that were fully aware and engaged in our day to day, and they spent most of the time assuring the other residents that what happened in #103 was totally fine.

At one point the management shifted, and the new manager, Nate, came to the door.

"Good morning, is Mr. Williams available?"

"No, sorry, he's in the hospital." I said.

"Yeah I heard that, we just need to catch up with him if possible."

"Ok I'll let him know when we talk to him. His brother is supposed to stop by and give us an update on his condition. I'm just here watching the place and his dog for him." I said.

He lightly peeked over my shoulder into the apartment and said, "Ok thanks."

Nate had to have been so confused. I mean Willie had been in the hospital for about two months, and after having met Willie, you'd be pressed to wonder how a guy his age had the kind of traffic and community of drug addicts stopping by that he did. Willie was about sixty-eight years old at the time, a total hippie, long grayed hair with a pony tail, and basically sat around vaping his weed and blowing lines. It was a fucking wonder that he wasn't in the hospital for a heart attack or stroke.

Finally it got to the point that my guy began selling heroin, and the traffic flow and company around the trap house got really questionable, even for my comfort zone. It became like a pawn shop, people were showing up with electronics and other oddball stuff asking to see the dealer. Could they get $20 of black for a $40 gift card? Could they steal a couple cases of beer and a bottle of liquor for a point or two? The door barely remained closed, and there were shopping carts full of random shit starting to be left outside of the building. The coke business was one thing, but when the boss started selling H, it brought all kinds of interest and questions about what went on at the end of our hall. I'm sure the safety of the whole building felt more compromised than usual.

Over those months I spent time using and dealing with all kinds of people; meeting folx in the area around lower Queen Anne and Belltown for the boss. One of the nights I left the apartment with another fellow to drop off some blow and black at a local strip club. We left the spot by Key Arena shortly before 10 p.m. and walked our way over to the Hurricane Cafe, stopping to have a drink and a couple games of pool; and then finally the call came in that the guys buying the dope were showing up at the club a few blocks away.

We made our way over, came in through the door, up the stairs and did the deal in a hallway that led down past some porno viewing rooms. We were asked if we wanted to have a couple drinks and lines, hanging out for a few. By this time I realized that the group I was dealing with were a handful of familiar gay men; nothing really alarming about that.

What was alarming was coming to, still in the same room that we got the drinks brought to us in, but as I turned my head from side to side I couldn't find the guy I came out to the club with to do the deal.

I found it awfully difficult to get my thoughts together; and just then I realized that something was happening down below my waistline. As I began to sit up, it became clear that there was another man going down on me. I sat up as quickly as I could, became very combative but couldn't get my footing, and the guy took off out of the room. I reached for my phone and money, fell over and checked my pocket for my stash, all of which were still present. Looking at my phone, it was sometime before 5 a.m. and I had been out of it for four or more hours; I couldn't wrap my head around what just happened.

I made my way out of the building, and still don't fully remember the walk back to the apartment. Most of it probably due to the disbelief that I had just been sexually assaulted by another man, but also that I had been drugged in order for this to occur. I walked myself back through all of the events of the evening, the best I could recall, and recounted my drug and alcohol consumption. I had only had five or six beers and a bunch of coke before walking on out to the Hurricane Cafe, surely not a recipe for drugging and sexual assault given my track record of substance intake. Something happened there between the cafe and the cocktails at the club. Fuck. This is crazy; unreal. I told myself, "This isn't the kind of thing that happens to men, right?" My own fear and remorse set in; this was something I wasn't going to tell anyone about. Ever.

Over the course of the next three weeks, Willie's physical abilities returned. He came back out of the hospital and was ready to take back over his apartment and the dope business. The building was supposedly up for sale and the trap shop wasn't going to be allowed a new lease, so I turned the phone on one day and said I had enough to my daughter's mother; and just like that, I left.

I started staying back at the apartment with Ione and Rachael, and we scraped by for the winter. Between her yoga teaching and some of my work, we landed a tax return that afforded us a trip to Hawaii. Her mom, sister and her kid were going, but my oldest brother had a large place on the big island that the girls and I could stay at, while her mom and sister stayed up in town. We caught up with friends that had moved there years earlier and explored the beaches; and overall it was a really good trip for a few days.

I took a drink on the second to last day, and I never came back in the morning to get in the car with everyone else. There had been an exchange of words the day prior in which my resentment festered into discomfort, and by the day of departure I was bent on drowning that resentment, and so I did. I returned two days later having to bump my flights and sleep on the beach because my brother's property was rented out based on our initial duration of stay.

Within a month after the trip, we had moved into another place further south, and my condition worsened. We were back into another farm season, and with that came the daily burn out that I would check out from with my drinking. Once again, I was on the road to and from the farm and was high almost every day.

I did have some free time during the days after processing orders and making customer contact, and Ione and I would spend the afternoons outdoors or with her working on her art. We played regularly at the parks, went swimming, explored and took trips to the city for kid events. I really enjoyed this time with her, especially since everyone else was just over me and my behaviors, frankly. Ione wasn't judgmental and just wanted to be with me; she was the last individual that didn't seem worn out.

Early in the morning one day in May, my daughter's mother got enraged with me for having been drinking the night before, and we started arguing. As per usual, things didn't end well, and after a push and pull with the front door, each of us trying to keep the other out, the door slammed shut, breaking one of her fingers, and she drove off to the hospital. Her mother came by an hour later to get my daughter, and I packed up some clothes to send my kid off with. I went on about completing my work for the day, and went out drinking that night.

The next morning there was a knock at the door, and I went and opened it. Two police officers were at the top of the stairwell.

"Are you Joe Conniff?" they asked.

"Yes." I said.

"Could you please step outside and speak with us?"

As I stepped out onto the landing, one of the officers turned me around.

"You're under arrest for assault."

I couldn't say anything, I was actually caught completely off guard since I had been smashed again last night, and had tried to drink away the events of the morning before.

Holy shit. I'm being arrested, and for all things considered in my past I'd have never expected to be arrested for assault or domestic violence for my first time.

10

TRP

I spent about two hours in a holding cell by booking and transfers with two other guys. They had us waiting for a couple of women, and then we would be making the thirty minute drive to the Regional Justice Center jail in Kent.

It was about 5:30 p.m. when we got ankle shackled and loaded into the transport van. I was sitting on the other side of the separation grate from a young woman, who couldn't have been much younger than me. We got to talking about why we were in and it turns out she was in drug court too. She shared some details about running and gunning with her boyfriend, having their motel door kicked in up in North Seattle by SPD, getting offered drug court, and now they were both doing the TRP program in Kent.

When we arrived at the jail they began to take the women to another entrance. As she was getting out, she said, "Hey can you tell Max I said hi please? He's my boyfriend, and he's in the unit you're going to. He's got a big owl tattooed on his forearm."

"Sure thing." I said.

We were given a couple of sack lunches, having missed the dinner service, and brought on down to Lincoln unit.

When I walked in I couldn't believe what I saw. I instantly recognized about twenty faces from Third Avenue and guys were yelling and waving at me. It was the first time in a while I felt like anyone was excited to see me. As I glanced around the more I realized Happy was right, so many of us from the block were here for the Transitional Recovery Program through drug diversion court.

There were two tiers, with individual cells. Two bunks in each, but only one person assigned to each cell. This was a good thing, I thought to myself. I won't be at the mercy of putting up with someone else's funkiness or them being at odds with me for any reason and having to share space. The only thing about the rooms were that there were a couple windows looking inward to the guard desk; no bars, so potentially a bit quieter; but if you get claustrophobic without the open air of steel bars, you were out of luck. There were a row of showers, a vending machine for pop and other junk foods, and two TV areas. One area had a bunch of tables where most guys shot the shit and played cards; the other area had about twenty-five chairs and a mounted TV stemming out from the top tier walkway. The unit also had its own yard-out attached to it. All of it was a far better situation than the yard-out at the downtown jail. This had steel bars and razor wire intertwined thirty feet above, but with that at least you were able to get some sunlight during the daytime. There was a basketball hoop, a couple pull up bars and a little sign that read, "19 laps around the yard=1 mile". The other solid improvement over being in custody downtown was that there was a bookshelf, and the literature was rotated weekly.

Right after I got situated I made the rounds catching up with everyone I knew. It was a relief to see some of them, but at the same time I was trying to understand how in the hell anything was going to work or change being locked down with the same exact people I had been getting loaded with in the streets. And if this place was anything like the downtown jail, there were sure to be drugs in the unit, and probably were already.

Before long, it was lights out, and I noticed six of the inmates were allowed to stay out past the rest of the unit for an extra hour or so. That's when I noticed Happy. He was one of the trustees and he had some extra privileges. I got my bunk made, grabbed a book, and settled in to what would be my new "house" for the next ninety and some odd days.

Breakfast goes down about 5:15-5:30 a.m. and the whole unit pretty much goes back to sleep until seven or eight. When I got up later that first morning, Happy had waved me over to the table he was sitting at to introduce me to a couple of other guys. As I reached over to shake one guy's hand, I noticed the owl inked into his arm.

Before he could introduce himself, I said, "Max right?"

"Yeah." he laughed, with a shred of concern in his eyes, "How'd you know that?"

"I was in the transport with a woman who said you'd be here."

He lit up and said, "Oh yeah! That's my girl, she had court in Seattle yesterday."

By now, most of the guys I knew from the street should have had a substantial amount of time abstinent from anything, unless they had used in the unit, which meant somebody had tucked some dope in their ass to get it in. Not saying that at a certain point in earlier jail stays I would have opted out of using that dope, but considering I didn't have the physical pull of being recently in withdrawal I found the idea of using in there less attractive. I spent the next few days catching up with people, but I noticed more and more that many of the guys I knew weren't expressing much about what drug court was doing for them, or what their plans towards staying clean were after release. This seemed kind of odd to me. A lot of them were coming and going from biweekly court hearings, and most just came back talking about housing options and release dates. I started thinking to myself, "I don't have a place to stay because I couldn't stop using fucking heroin, and I sure as hell won't manage to get a place if I can't stay stopped."

As I paid more attention to what guys like Max and Happy were doing, which were only a handful of individuals, I realized that these guys talked about the twelve step meetings coming into the unit two nights a week, and what they were getting out of the classes. They discussed their plans around housing, structure and stability, and staying away from the people, places and things that got us here; including our thought patterns. It dawned on me that these few individuals were people that I was sure had similar experiences with drugs and alcohol that I did, and weren't as obsessed with talking about how to live that life better or not get caught this time around; but were actually focused on keeping the cognitive tools and applying the skills and understanding they were learning about themselves and their be-haviors. This was the shit I needed to figure out how to do.

Problem was I wouldn't start the in-custody treatment pro-gramming for another two or three weeks. I still needed to have a chemical dependency assessment and wait for space to free up in the groups. In the meantime, I figured I better stay close to Happy and Max and start working on boundaries with people immediately. I managed to score myself a bible, an AA 12 Steps and 12 Traditions, and a book on meditation, breathing and yoga practices for folx behind bars called "We're All Doing Time" by Bo Lozoff.

Attendance at the AA meetings in the unit was strongly en-couraged if you were in drug court programming, so I started hit-ting those. The Thursday meeting was a little inconsistent, but the Tuesday one with these two guys, Fred and Joe, was spot on, every time.

Fred had actually spent a couple months in the RJC some eleven years earlier, after his last go around with a DUI and drug charge. He was really open about his experiences which rang sim-ilar to my current state of affairs. Plus, I thought there was some-thing truly incredible about a guy that had been through this shit and would willingly walk back through these doors to bring a meeting to people he had never met.

I started sharing and opening up in the meetings, but for the most part a lot of the other guys didn't say much. Everyone has their reasons, whether it be needing to listen for the similarities, being shy or just feeling mandated to do this work leading toward a life they weren't ready for. I didn't care. All I understood at the time was that if I was going to change the direction of my life, shit needed to start right now, in this jail.

I was having a hard time understanding the 12 Steps and 12 Traditions without the context of the Big Book and a sponsor, and per Fred and Joe, they didn't have a good stream of literature resources for the jails and institutions service. I really wanted to understand the process as outlined in the Big Book so the steps would make more sense, so Fred asked me to stay committed to hitting the meetings for a couple more weeks and stay after chatting with him and Joe, and he would be sure to get me a Big Book when one became available.

I had been reading the bible steadily and was hoping to get some relief from that and prayer, but honestly I struggled with my faith in a higher power associated with religion, which was my only basis of understanding. With all the suffering my mother had endured, all the deaths in my family with cancer, and all the shit I had gone through in the last decade, I had a really hard time understanding how surrender to a God or a deeper belief was going to change my situation. Plus, my mother was extremely committed to her faith, which confused the hell out of me; wondering how she could continue to suffer in pain that much and remain hopeful and committed to a higher power. I really felt like I needed to take some action in my life and begin to understand myself and why I did things the way I did. I will say that I found a lot of wisdom in the Bible's proverbs and they provided much needed inspiration in aligning values, ethics and character at a time when I completely lacked all three of those. I would also go on to learn much more about the purpose and intent of my mother's faith and spirituality once I learned enough about the role that doubt played in my thought patterns and ambivalence in establishing a relationship to a higher power.

With my disinterest in a seemingly typical Christian approach, I was working with a lot of anxiety at this time around how my path forward would look in the twelve steps with the higher power piece. The breathing practices and yoga routines were helping with the anxiety, but I didn't yet have a basis for correlation on connecting a recovery process to yoga and meditation in the long run. Also, I was starting to do brief mindfulness of breathing sits of eight to ten minutes, which can seem like a fucking eternity in jail. The thing was, when I did the sits I got more freedom and relief in those few minutes than I'd ever found in a line of blow or hit of heroin.

One night while we were beginning evening rack-out, the doors opened with new guys coming to the unit, and in walked Brian from the day I was getting ready to agree to go to the TRP at court. Apparently, he decided to kick dope in the community on warrant, rather than in custody, then turned himself in to do the program. This was great, another welcome face to add to the mix. Plus Brian presented a little more focused than some of the other guys, so I figured he might be down to jump in on this serious recovery business with the couple of us.

The same week that I finally began intensive outpatient programming, Fred came in with a Big Book for me. I started in on the first 164 pages and blew through them twice in a week. Everything in the chapter's The Doctor's Opinion, More about Alcoholism, and most everything else for that matter, jumped right out at me. This is me. This is the way I drink and use. I needed this to work, somehow. The Twelve Step stuff, the yoga, mindfulness and meditation, all of it.

By the second week of the treatment programming, I was really appreciating the fact that I had all this time to focus on myself and my behaviors. The classes were great because we were hashing out little bits of Cognitive Behavioral Therapy, examining boundaries and triggers, and had a separate day committed to MRT (Moral Reconation Therapy) which is a workbook that employs humility and ownership of one's actions while asking the participants to closely follow simple directions for completing the steps in the workbook. One progresses through the book by presenting to the group's peers and not deviating from the process outlined to complete each step. Some require basic stick figure pictures to be drawn to represent pieces of one's life, others have goals and interpersonal relationships to be assessed, evaluated and refined before moving onward. Kind of a nice precursor to other work related to the process of recovery and modifying one's unskillful behaviors.

With the class kicking off my mornings Monday through Friday, I would come back to the unit and have about fifteen minutes of rack-out before heading back into my cell for a couple of hours. Once back in my cell, I had about an hour and fifteen minutes before lunch. I used the first thirty-five minutes back in to lay my blanket out on the floor, do a yoga asana routine I had pieced together from the Bo Lozoff book, and follow that up with fifteen minutes of various breathing exercises followed by five to ten minutes of mindfulness meditation. Shortly after lunch, we would get a rack-out and I would use another forty-five minutes to exercise, do pull ups and a couple hundred push-ups.

By this point both Max and Happy were trustees, and they were getting extra lunches and trays at meal time. They were overwhelmingly generous to me with the extra food and I was starting to gain weight in a healthy manner rather quickly. Considering that I had come into jail at around 130 pounds, having been at almost 175 before going all in on heroin, this was the beginning of the best I had felt physically since my weightlifting days while in the Navy.

After lunch, I would finish my workouts by grabbing six or seven of the biggest books off the shelves, run them into my cell and do arm curls with them wrapped up in my pillow case. To finish the afternoon I would read other random non-fiction books, the AA 12 and 12, and take a brief nap.

Dinner would go down about 4:30 or 5 p.m. and we would rack-out for the evening from about 6:30-9 p.m. Over the course of the evening, Max, Happy, Brian and I would do a good 100 pull ups, 200-300 push-ups and shoot the shit in between. The nights the meetings came in a couple of us would attend those as well. After rack-back at 9 p.m. I would dig in on the Big Book for about an hour, highlighting what I found relevant, and follow that up with another 15-20 minutes of mindfulness and meditation practices.

One afternoon, one of the corrections officers asked if we had any veterans in the unit, and if so to come to the guard station. I thought to myself for a few about this and decided to say yes. Even though I had been booted out close to the end of my enlistment, I figured what the hell, I had done a couple tours and sure did my share of service.

I approached the guard desk first.

"What branch?' he asked.

"Navy." I said.

"It's not as cool as the Army but you served; that's good enough." as he laughed he rolled up his sleeve and showed me an Army Airborne tattoo. By this time there were a handful of other guys that had come up, but I had never really conversed with any of them.

"Check this out; so there's a pilot program for veterans that will begin to take place in this unit a few days a week. There will be different programs offered. Some will be geared towards resources, a writing workshop, and some kind of mindfulness session. There will also be a couple VA staff members coming in to meet with y'all one day a week regarding your benefits, eligibility and other service related info. Are you tracking?"

"Yes." we all said in unison. It was cool, all of the sudden there was this old familiar brotherhood present that I had been unaware of in the unit, one of them being the officer.

"Alright, if you're interested in any of it, head on back to the programming room and sign in. They'll give you the schedule."

When I went into the room, I looked at the offerings, and immediately asked to be put in for the Saturday afternoon mindfulness meditation group.

11

King Heroin

I was brought to the holding cell at the Des Moines police station before being transported over to SCORE (South Correctional Entity) Jail for the afternoon, and I stayed there into the late evening. A couple hours shy of midnight I was moved over to the King County Correctional Facility in downtown Seattle. The good news was that I would likely see a judge the next day on the afternoon calendar.

I was initially charged with assault in the second degree, but it was quickly brought to the third degree and they were looking to move forward with an assault in the fourth (DV) by the time I got out of the courtroom. The significant challenge is that there was now a no-contact order and I had no place to stay.

One of the farm guys picked me up and gave me a van to use to continue bringing in the restaurant sales for the business. A day or two later I was able to get a police escort to get my things from the house, and again I packed my pool cues and my clothes and threw them into the work van. All that was left of my life fit in a single bag, once again. The place that the farm crew was staying at had no space available for me to sleep, so I spent about three weeks living out of the van in the Burien area, south of Seattle. I made less trips to Yakima, as my daughter's mother ceased her farm work involvement given the no-contact order, so I was able to make the case for needing to be available locally for customer service and order processing. I did the majority of my work from the library, since most of it was done via email and thumb drives, along with some phone and in-person contact as needed. I spent the mornings getting cleaned up and showered at the YMCA, and I picked up a couple days working the farmers markets so I could get some fresh fruits and veggies as well as lunch, and I would get paid out in cash at the end of the day.

By late afternoon, I would work from the local bar for an hour on my laptop before eating there and getting loaded for the evening; usually passing out in the van in the side parking lot until it was time to go to the YMCA again in the morning.

After a few weeks my buddy Cameron, the bartender at my regular drinking spot, came over to get my order.

"Hey man, I heard you've been living out of your van. Is that true?"

"Yeah pretty much, at least for the time being." I said.

We had a brief exchange that lasted about four or five minutes, and I came away with a possible place to stay. He offered to talk to his roommate Chris, and see if I could stay over there for a while.

By the next afternoon, Chris was at the bar and freely offered me to stay there for a month or more while I figured my shit out.

Staying with Chris and Cameron opened my eyes to a whole other world that they were living in between work hours. Chris smoked meth and stayed up for a couple days at a time, and

Cameron was smoking heroin, which I had actually tried with him a handful of times in the months prior.

Once I started staying there, their friend Leo was always around, and he was the guy. Leo sold heroin, crystal and coke, and used all three, all day. He practically lived there half time and any money that came into that house went to Leo, and he was generous with his dope, so there were always foils of black, lines of coke or bubbles of meth going around.

While all this was going on, the court ordered me to CCAP Basic (Community Center for Alternative Programs), which was like daily reporting while awaiting sentencing, and all I had to do was call in Monday through Friday before 10 a.m. leave a voicemail for my assigned case worker Will, and I had to follow that protocol for 60 days, nothing more, until further notice.

During those two months, I developed quite the heroin habit. I was still doing coke, occasional meth, but I used heroin from sun up to sun down. Due to my work with the markets and the amount of hours I was able to log, I constantly had cash and was able to afford to always keep dope on me. I spent less and less on blow, and heroin became my focus.

When I was ordered to CCAP Basic, the case mentioned that I had been drinking the night before the incident with Rachael, so there were some conditions that I was likely alcohol dependent and I was told by the attorney I ought to figure out how to stop drinking. Nothing was mentioned about other drugs, but it was possible that I could get pulled into the CCAP office for a breathalyzer at any time. Heroin immediately replaced alcohol as my constant go to for self-medication. It had relative effects, and the truth was that I was in so much pain about my life, cocaine held less interest because hypervigilance and alertness were no longer serving me. Heroin kept me numb and calmed, making life itself slightly more tolerable. Between my heroin use and being welcomed at Chris's place, I felt warmth and belonging, something that had been missing for some time.

Opiates are not just helpful for physical discomfort, they also work really well on emotional pain; probably the reason I wasn't drawn to my mom's pills earlier along. Back then I just didn't feel like I was totally hopeless, but that feeling had really settled in as of recently. There was always the impending doom of the harvest season ending, and I would be out of money again. But for now, I'm just going to roll with this. My thinking was "just let me get through today this way, and tomorrow I'll change things"; I had resigned myself to coping by using heroin, and due to its stranglehold on my life, the tomorrows of change never came.

My reality after the charge had become excruciating. I hadn't seen my daughter in over two months, I was practically homeless, and I only worked to afford to buy the drugs I used to check out of life more frequently than ever before. After about two months of me living there, Cameron's habit had gotten so bad that he and Chris had a falling out and it was time for me to go. I started staying at motels on Pacific Highway, meeting Leo over the course of my work days, and nodding off alone in shitty motel rooms at night.

By August, my daughter's mother reached out, and I swore I stopped drinking. Even though we had the no contact order and the sentencing still hadn't happened, as far as alcohol was concerned I truly wasn't drinking. I was able to see Ione, and I was able to still keep dope on me, but I used just enough to keep my body going, and not feel the physical pull of withdrawal. This period of a month had me back doing a couple runs to the farm and I was able to keep the heroin use under the radar as I slowly eased my way back into living at the apartment, part time. I would use a little more after everyone went to bed, and I was out the door early the next day.

Eventually the sentence had been passed, Gross Misdemeanor, DV Assault in the Fourth Degree, and I was ordered to do some outpatient treatment and a Moral Reconation Therapy workbook over the coming months. I actually went to the classes at CCAP for about two weeks, sneaking dope into the facility in my shoe so when we went on lunch I could run to the park and smoke just enough heroin to make it through the afternoon without feeling ill.

Finally the day arrived again when the season was coming to an end, the money was running out; and my habit was around $150 of heroin daily.

On this particular weekend, Leo was unable to meet me on a Saturday afternoon, and by Sunday morning I was sick as hell. For the first time ever, I was officially in withdrawal. I had never experienced this in the last seven months, not one time. My daughter, her mother and I were scheduled to go somewhere and I couldn't physically hold my head up; I was sneezing, dry heaving and sweating my ass off, and shaking with the chills. After the years of my unreliability, Rachael wasn't having it this time.

She finally looked at me, with my daughter next to her and said, "Joe, what the fuck is going on?"

I started rocking back and forth with my head in my hands, thinking about what I can do to get out of here, right now, and get some fucking dope. It was all I could think about, and I had $60 in my pocket; I just needed to create an out and find a place to score some heroin. It was also Sunday which meant it was pay-day, the last one of the season, if I could meet the boss some-where in the city; I just had to get well first. Leo's phone had been off since he said he ran out the day before, and it had only been sixteen hours since my last use but I felt like I was dying.

"Joe, answer me!" she demanded.

I looked up briefly and shouted, "I'm a fucking heroin ad-dict!

After admitting that for the first time, I immediately felt sicker than before. I shuffled over to put my shoes and jacket on, and took off out the door to the bus stop.

What the fuck did I just say? I can't believe I just heard myself say that. It's really falling apart now, isn't it?

I didn't even know where I was going. I just needed to not be bothered so that I could figure out where I could put my $60 to use and get right.

I took the 156 bus to Southcenter and caught the next avail-able route into Downtown Seattle. I had heard of The Blade, which was considered to be the largest open air drug market in the Pacific Northwest. I got off the bus, and within three minutes a guy caught onto my wandering dope-sick gaze and asked how much money I had. He gave me a couple methadone tablets for $10 and we started making laps looking for a dealer.

It didn't take long to score some shit, and once that was done, I felt relieved that this kind of place existed. I mean you could just walk down Third Avenue between Pike and Pine and basi-cally ask anyone, "Got any black?" and they would either say yes or take you to somebody who was holding. After getting well in an alley by I-5 and Marion Street, I called my boss and asked to meet up and get my check. Lucky for me, he was on his way to Pike Place just around the corner from The Blade.

Right after I got my check, I turned around and went back to Third Ave and spent another $120 on heroin. I finally landed at a hotel in Renton and stayed there with the remainder of my paycheck for a day and a half. After the money and dope ran out, I got up the nerve to call Rachael and said I needed to talk to her.

We met at the Burien Transit Center in the evening, and I walked up to the car and said, "I'm sorry; this is what's going on, and I need help. I need to be done with this shit."

"What do we do?" she asked.

"I don't know, but it's gonna kill me if I don't stop."

I spent the next couple weeks at the apartment on and off, and managed to scrape together some money. It wasn't money that should have gone to me, but I scraped it together nevertheless.

Two farm seasons prior I had asked for a substantial raise to be compensated for the revenue the wholesale business had brought in. One of the years had produced well over $500,000 of previously unseen revenue, and I was only making $12/hr. Both Rachael and I felt that the compensation was unjust, and this is just one example of how resentments fester and I would act out on them through substance use. This would also be my first venture in needing to get deeply creative in funding my heroin addiction to survive. I knew that the farm had not yet been paid for some of the late season invoices, and I went on to collect the outstanding balances for myself.

It worked for a while, until my behavior and urgency raised questions with a wholesale account and they called the farm manager. So after that plan came crashing down, I was out of options. As much as I wanted to fix things and get clean, what the fuck was I going to use to cope with the damage and destruction in my life? There was no way anybody could walk through this wreckage and clean it up sober. Not possible.

So off I went. I made a call to one of the guys I met out on The Blade, old man Mark. He lived up on Aurora in a rundown apartment complex by 87th. He was in his early 50's and used a cane from a back injury years earlier. Since the cane made him vulnerable to getting robbed out on the block, he had me start working with him as his back up and lookout when he came downtown to sell his dope.

Mark's girlfriend, Pam, had worked Aurora Avenue in the sex trade years earlier. She was ok with me crashing out at their place, especially since I was helping Mark move his product. Both she and Mark had very heavy habits, and most days their place was a dope shooting gallery. Many of the other young women working Aurora would come in and out to get tips on navigating the sex work from Pam and score dope from Mark.

For everyone who ever came by that place, it was about survival. Most of the women that came by had been sexually, physically, or emotionally beaten down. Many of them had it happen in their childhoods.

Outside of conversing with the women, I never hooked up with any of them. For me, everything was about the conversations. It was amazing, the lives that some of these people had lived. Many of them had done incredible things in their past, or held really intriguing occupational positions at some point. Some of them had been homeowners or they were parents that had their children taken away due to their use. Somewhere at the bottom of everything was a disconnect and/or trauma that occurred in their formative years or later on. And the life they lived now? Unfortunately, that's a whole other trauma in and of itself.

Sarah was one of these women. Mark and Pam's place was a good size studio but there was only a bed, couch and a full-size, low rise bed over in the corner that doubled as a sofa during the day. I usually crashed on the couch, and Sarah on the full. She would go out and work Aurora during the day and was usually done by 7 or 8 p.m. calling it a night. I often went out in the evenings to try and sell a little in the neighborhood for Mark and see what all the talk over the years regarding Aurora Ave in Seattle had really been about.

Aurora Avenue is like a physical and emotional battlefield. There are victims and perpetrators, dealers, consumers, shootings, stabbings, all sorts of ups and downs. Theft, robbery, assault and overdose are all too common up there. The stretch from 80th that included Mark's up to 130th was the worst in my opinion. At the time I met Mark and Pam, The Orion Motel was by far one of the most toxic places people convened on that stretch of road. At 125th and Aurora, The Orion had so much dope and violence coming out of it that it seemed the cops and medics were always there. One of our friends, Shy, a big guy from Chicago, got stabbed in the shoulder there picking up rock for some of us. When he came through the door with the dope he ran into the bathroom and started patching himself up like it was nothing. Just wrong place, wrong time on a random ass Tuesday night in North Seattle.

In December, one of the women working the avenue came pounding on the door. As she was smashing on the entry, we could hear car tires squealing on the back street parallel to Aurora that butted up against the back of the apartment.

Pam ran over and grabbed the door, shoved her in and told her to sit down and shut up. Pam appeared composed and seemed to have been familiar with the looks and sounds of whatever the hell was going down. After the sound of the revved engine and screeching tires finally disappeared, Pam approached her to find out what all had gone down.

"Heidi, you need to tell me what happened, right now." Pam said.

"This john beat the fuck out of me a week or two ago, and I got his ass back." she said.

"What do you mean 'got him back'?"

"He picked me up again and I saw where he keeps his cash, lots of it. I ripped him off this morning and he's after me. He just saw me at the gas station, and drove over the fucking curb towards me, so I ran here. I'm sorry! It's the only place I could go." she exclaimed.

The Shell station was only two blocks west of Mark and Pam's. Pam didn't seem startled by any of this, and there wasn't much she hated more than a physically abusive client.

Pam asked, "Ok, Jesus; how much did you get him for?"

"$7,000." Heidi said.

"Jesus Christ, no wonder he's after you! Fuck, Heidi."

Heidi pulled out the cash, counted out a grand and put it on the table.

"Pam can I please stay here, just for a couple days? You can have this, I just need a place for a few days, until I can figure something out."

Mark and Pam had a brief side chat in the kitchen and came back.

"Sure, but you are absolutely not walking out the door here until we know where you can go long term after this. You can't go back out on Aurora, you know that right?"

"Yes." Heidi said.

Once Heidi knew she could stay, she asked Pam and Mark to call their dealers and get a shit ton of dope. Mark and I ended up going out to pick it all up, and Shy stayed back with the women.

The next few days turned into a free-for-all at that apartment. There were rigs, foil and pipes all over the place, people half out of it and falling over trying to stick spikes in their arms, bleeding and bruising, hoping to hit a vein. Heidi probably blew through a good $3000 in forty-eight hours, and she was paying for everyone to get high.

Mark had his regulars coming by, and we still had to sell on The Blade for a couple hours a day. The regular women from the track were coming and going as usual, and word had traveled between the sex workers that this guy was looking for Heidi.

Shy went out to The Orion to see if anyone could help in finding a safe place for her and get her out of Mark and Pam's; he returned about an hour later.

"Hey we need to get her the fuck out of here tonight. I have a friend that will take her down to Tacoma for a few days, and get her on a bus to some friends in Portland by Wednesday. Word is out that she's been here and a few other places and there's a crew looking for her. It's not good. One of the other girls must have said something about the crazy money being spent down at the Way West apartments. That motherfucker is hot about that $7,000." said Shy.

Two hours later, we had Heidi in a car with Shy and they rolled out to Tacoma. Shy, in his 6'2 intimidating self, was playing bodyguard until she got on that bus to Portland.

The rest of the night at Mark and Pam's was fairly quiet. There were a few regulars, and I did a couple of off-site meets for Mark at the gas station.

The next day, Mark and I headed out early to sell down on The Blade. By mid-afternoon, we were sold out and we headed back up on the E-Line to re-up. We met our guy at Greenwood and 105th, and headed back to the apartment to make some food with Sarah and Pam.

Around 9:30 p.m. there was a knock at the door, and Mark had just come in from walking their Jack Russel puppy, Toby and was hanging the leash next to the door.

"Who is it?" Mark asked.

A woman's voice said, "It's Jessie."

"Ok, one sec." Mark said. Jessie was a regular woman that typically stopped by after she set out on the track to work for the evening.

As soon as Mark flipped the deadbolt and turned the knob, the door burst open and Mark flew onto his back, landing next to me on the sofa. Jessie got pushed to the side and three large guys came through the door.

"Nobody fucking move, where's the girl; where's the dope?"

There were four huge Pacific Islanders; two of them were moving through the small apartment, and the two blocking the door and standing over Mark and I had pistols pointed at us.

"She's gone." said Pam. We don't know where the hell she went."

One guy kept the gun on Mark while he shook him down, taking most of the dope we had just picked up in Greenwood. One of the other ones was moving through the place and came over and rummaged through my shit, ran my pockets and took the $8 fucking dollars I had left, not finding anything else of interest, and walked out the door. The other three guys followed.

I stayed at Mark and Pam's that one last night, and didn't get shit for sleep. I couldn't let go of the thought that maybe somebody else had been tipped off and was planning on stopping by too. I had maybe $20 worth of dope left and needed to figure out what I could do or where I could stay. I couldn't spend another night at their place after the robbery, risking losing what little I had left of my life.

12

Life on the Edge of the Blade

When I got up the next morning, I was able to get a call into my sister, making up a story about how I needed money to pay for a week to stay on my friend's couch, and she wired me $80. What I told her was the furthest from the truth, as I was preparing myself to live on the streets in downtown Seattle.

I did what dope I had left to get started in on the day, and rolled down to Money Tree on Third Avenue to pick up the cash. I thanked Mark and Pam before leaving, and told them I just couldn't do this anymore, given the thought of being robbed again at gunpoint, or worse.

My intention was to take the $80, buy a gram, and pack it out into $10 bags and just keep turning it over. The idea was that I could do this a few times a day, stay well and be able to pull together enough money to rent another cheap motel room for a week, and just keep going like this until who knows when.

That whole time I had naturally been on warrant for not attending the CCAP classes, and to be honest I really didn't fucking care. The only thing I could think about was the next bag, the next hit and the next sale, so I could do it all over again.

Over those couple months with Mark, I had gotten to know every dealer, every buyer, where to get black, crack and crystal. Another Blade veteran taught me how to stash hold your shit so you could get through a shake down by the police by wearing boxer briefs or tighty whities and keeping the dope in a pill bottle stashed next to your package.

I hatched out my whole plan with the money from my sister almost seamlessly, and things went smooth for a couple of days. I felt a sense that I could do this for weeks, months, or maybe even longer. Not because I wanted to, but just because I thought I could in an effort to survive and keep on using.

There is this strange concept of freedom that comes with being out there running in the game on the streets. I remember hearing a talk from dharma teacher Noah Levine about "freedom from and freedom to", and the difference that exists between them. Similarly as he described in the talk I absolutely had the freedom to do whatever the hell I wanted to, but by no means did I have any freedom from; and in my case it meant not having freedom from the bondage of substances and addiction

It had been well over three months since the last time I had snorted a line of coke. Everything out here on the Blade was crack cocaine only. As for other substances, you could get everything from Xanax to Suboxone, marijuana to methadone, and anything else in between. All of it was available on a 250 yard stretch between Pike and Pine Streets, even though there were a surrounding nine and a half blocks that had been identified by Seattle PD as a high drug trafficking area, mainly because many of us moved around and slept in the vicinity of the Blade. Average folx walked on by like they didn't see us; and Seattle PD and/or security officers often criminalized our homeless aspects by waking and moving us out of empty doorways, stairwells or anywhere that one could find a place to sit down and close their eyes. Countless times I came back to get my bed roll and blanket, stashed under a loading dock and out of the way, only to find a security guard tearing my stuff up or throwing it in a dumpster.

The stretch in front of the Hard Rock Cafe and Target that led up past the lounge towards Walgreens was primarily where the crack dealers hung out. Looking more closely at everything in the drug trafficking area, one could almost relate its appearance to that of a farmers or flea market. There were specific areas that had concentrations of particular activities; everything from the sale and use of narcotics to the trading of goods.

I managed to take on a steady flow of sales daily, and I was able to keep myself well for the most part. My biggest downfall was my affinity for cocaine once I got just right on heroin. The crack head rush mixed with the euphoria of the heroin high was the perfect blend of medicine to really push aside the tragedy of my life as I was living it. Often times I would start chasing the coke high so much that I would trade or sell off my heroin to get crack, often realizing too late that I didn't put aside enough black to get well the next morning; becoming considerably screwed.

I know many times over the years in different settings and treatment intakes people ask questions like, "What's your drug of choice?" There's a problem there for me with that question. See drugs of choice for me are things like Ibuprofen or Benadryl; I can choose whether or not I will take them. But towards the end, every other substance that is an illicit narcotic became my "drug of no choice"; meaning I didn't have a choice in what drug or how much of one I used; I would use anything, at all costs, so long as it could change the way I related to the distress in my life.

In mid-January, I was smoking meth in the alley behind the Melbourne Tower with a couple of guys, and the cops came cruising in in their patrol SUV's. I knew I couldn't get out of there when they blocked the north and south ends of the alley.

"Alright guys, you know you're not supposed to be back here. We don't give a damn what you're doing, and when we run warrants if you're clear, you can go." one of the officers said.

Shit, the warrant, I thought.

Sure enough, when it was my turn, I stood there contemplating bolting, but figured I wouldn't make it far.

"Alright Mr. Conniff, turn around. You've got a warrant out for your arrest."

This time, I did a week in the county kicking dope on that bench warrant return, saw the judge, and was given one more shot at reporting to CCAP and completing the classes.

Right when I got out on a Friday afternoon, I walked up to The Blade and bumped into old man Mark.

"Aw that sucks man, you just got out today? Here's a few points, go and get right and hit me back later this week." he said.

Like it was meant to be. I knew I needed to be back at CCAP on Monday, but fuck. If I can use a tiny bit and get back on selling, maybe I can hold it together to make it through the groups. Sure, the dream of many addicts; let me show you how my way is going to work and somehow be different this time.

I made it through the weekend as planned with sales alright, except I never stopped using. When I got to CCAP, my old caseworker Will was there to check in with me.

He reviewed the court paperwork, looked up and said, "So what's going on? Are we going to try this again?"

"Yeah, I guess. It's going to be tough, I'm living out of doors, down here on the Blade." I said.

"You using? You know you aren't going to be able to use and do this, right?

"I know." I said.

He sighed and asked, "Ok, you remember where the class is, and the IOP group with Jerry down the hall after that, correct?"

"Yep."

Not even 30 minutes into the first group, I was pulled out for nodding off. The facilitator brought me into another room, dug a tiny flashlight out of his pocket and shined it into my eyes.

"Let's go see your caseworker." he said.

When we got back to Will's office, I sat outside while the facilitator caught him up on what happened in class.

"Joe, come on in."

I sat down, not knowing what was going to happen next. Are they calling an officer to come and take me back to county? I really had no clue how they handled this kind of thing.

"I want to help you man, I really do. But I can't do that if you're nodding off in class. You follow?"

"I do, and I'm sorry. My fucking life is a mess. I don't know how to stop, or how to pick up the pieces and get my shit together." I said.

"Come back tomorrow, try to be a little better prepared, and we'll refer you to some services that may be able to help get you started on something. We'll look at some treatment options and housing programs." he said.

"Ok, thanks Will."

By that afternoon once I was back out on the Blade I decided I wasn't going to go back to CCAP the next day. As scared as I was of the way I was living, I was also too fucking scared to stop. This was all I knew.

It was still incredibly cold outside during those winter months of 2015. I struggled many days needing to ensure I had enough heroin to forget about the discomfort of the elements. The ability to continue to get hotel rooms at the end of the day had long since become unrealistic because the only thing that really mattered to me was not running out of heroin. I didn't care where I was, inside or outside, just as long as I could drift off to a place that seemingly felt warm and tranquil; that's what heroin did for me.

Being homeless in downtown Seattle requires specific skill-sets, some illegal and some natural, to actually survive out here. Being knowledgeable of the mission services, restrooms you can access, and food opportunities were paramount in my experience.

I had found a stoop in front of a Mexican restaurant in Post Alley behind Pike Place Market that became my spot for the next two months. I never stayed there during the day, surely not during business hours. But after closing at 10 p.m. I knew nobody else really had any business or good sense to be down at that end of the alley, and I could be at whatever peace I could find in a cup of noodles, foil of black tar heroin, rock of crack cocaine and a 32 oz. beer. That to me, was the measure of a good day in my life as an addict. A truly superb day was having a wake up hit of H and a bag or two to sell to get the next day off on the right foot. These were now the finer things in my life. After some time, when the restaurant owner would leave at night, if he saw me coming down the alley he'd say, "Watch my place for me!" I think his cleaning crews told him about me, since they'd step over me most mornings to go in and prep the place for the day. They were pretty cool and never messed with me for being there. Sometimes they'd even bring out a cup of water or leave granola bars next to me; and I'd be gone by 7 a.m. leaving no trace that I had been there.

I'd pack up the bed roll I scored from a friend, stash it somewhere that I figured no one would mess with it, and make my way up to Pike Place to hit the restrooms and get well.

I had been running around with a couple of people that I could count on to bring me new sales, usually people that came down to the Blade for the same reasons that I ended up out there. Somebody else who had gotten hooked, flopped out, and burnt all the bridges and heard this is where all the junkies go. Outside of those, I had a steady stream of regulars that I dealt with the first half of the day.

Soon after I got out from the CCAP warrant, somebody introduced me to Brad. He had really good dope, but got paranoid and didn't like being out there for more than an hour at a time. After he saw how many people I knew and could sell to, he offered to put me on every morning. All I had to do was have $20 in hand, and he would set me up with a gram or two, and I could pay him back the difference throughout the course of the day.

During this time working for Brad, I would move forty to fifty dime bags by 11 a.m. and had a habit of about two to two and a half grams per day. The E-line bus would pull up to Third

Ave and Pike St and all the other folx that came down off of Aurora and out of the motels were there to sell or buy their dope. If you knew the right people and what to look for, you could make the loop around Third and Fourth between Pike and Pine and encounter thirty to forty dealers.

Street-side over in front of Starbucks, Walgreens and the IGA Market was where you could fence stolen property. There would be strings of people with shopping bags and a line of potential buyers dipping their hands and heads into the bags, deciding if they wanted it and haggling over what they'd be willing to pay. Many of the local business and chain retailers suffered at the hands of what my community and its people were doing to survive out here. Some of the common things of value were clothing, specifically Levi's 501 jeans, and cologne/perfume, electronics, and laundry detergent pods. This underground economy included every class, race and walk of life; in case anyone needs a reminder that addiction doesn't discriminate.

Most of the stolen goods came from Pacific Place, shops on Fifth Ave, Macy's, Brooks Brothers, Target, and anywhere else somebody could make a safe break for the door. There were vendors inside of Pike Place Market that you could sell stolen goods to, as well as fence to the employees at Joe's Market on Second and Pine, and the teriyaki shop at Second and Pike. All over this area regular people and small businesses were waiting for and/or willing to pay for boosted products, paying pennies on the dollar to and exploiting people like me who did whatever we could for the next hit of relief. Most of them were caught onto by the end of 2015 and shut down but the fucking racket that existed to feed Seattle's downtown addicted population was purely astonishing.

Some of it is still going on, but not anywhere close to what it was like five years ago.

I came to know many people while I was out there. Some of these folx I might run with for a few days, and we would hustle together. During this time I heard the background of almost every addicted person I encountered. It was difficult not to get the story of how people ended up bottomed out, chasing dope, trying to escape some kind of hurt or pain, only to create more in the process.

I love all of these people, honestly, and I'm quite sure I couldn't have survived out there without these connections. Somehow, this subculture that exists within the networks of addicts serves a sole purpose. As disconnected from society as one can get after years of substance abuse, this was the only thing keeping me going every day. The ability to have a community of people that suffered the way I did, that knew the challenges of the way I lived life, this was the common denominator that tied us all together, and really the only thing that I felt separated us from the rest of society. We truly understood each other, and more often than not, were willing to help one another out.

The people I stayed around while I was out there were more thoughtful and compassionate than some humans I've met over the years. The first night I ever slept out in a doorway, I was shivering trying to shelter myself from the cold wind rolling in off of Elliot Bay. I remember this guy David came over and threw me a blanket and then covered me with the remainder of his. Another friend used to come find me in the afternoon to hit the burrito stand by Pike, where the guy working would hook us up with a plate of food before shift change. A lot of the heroin users would do damn near anything to keep those they knew from having to be in withdrawal, and most of the ones I knew were generous with anything they had.

I believe many addicted and homeless populations living out of doors just get it; you can't really make it alone in this world. They have no delusion about that. Yes, as addicts we can absolutely be greedy and self-centered, probably because we feel people don't understand us, why we do what we do. But once we get around other addicts, we know we're home. We know we'll fucking die alone in any other pocket of society. People experience joy and happiness on multiple levels; but to suffer, to be in pain, everybody understands what that shit's like. Nothing brings people closer together than the shared experiences of pain.

Word on the street had been traveling that there was a big bust coming. We had heard there were undercovers, confidential informants, and you couldn't help but notice the extra police and sheriff bike patrols. Plus, the drug dealing and trafficking of stolen property were so easy for any regular commuter or citizen to see; we knew it was just a matter of time.

One day, towards the end of February I rolled up onto the block with Joey, and another guy that used to come see me in the afternoons. Somebody stopped to talk to Joey, and I did a quick sale, and kicked Joey down a few bucks for the hook up, and the other guy and I took off to see the crack dealers.

When we rounded the corner at Walgreens, five sheriff's department bike cops rolled up on us. I tried to tell my guy to move out closer to the street, but as we did, they moved in on us.

"Ok guys, let's see some ID." my stomach fucking dropped. I had the CCAP warrant, and about twenty bags of dope in a pill bottle on me.

As I reached for my wallet I asked, "What's this about?"

The officer pulled out his notepad, "Well, we got a call about a guy in a two-toned grey hoodie with a bandana who is suspected of ripping off some Beats Audio headphones from Target. You happen to be wearing a two-toned grey hoodie and bandana."

"Got it." I said, and handed him my ID. The guy I was with handed over his.

"No history of theft, got it." one of the officers said into the radio. There was a little more chatter and the other officer gave me the rundown on how they got the call about the headphones.

When the one that was on the radio came back, he told the officer in charge that dispatch reported I had a warrant out of CCAP.

"Alright, here's the deal Mr. Conniff. You have a warrant for a CCAP violation, but we're not out here for that today. You came up clean on a theft history, so we're gonna let you go. You need to get down to the courthouse and CCAP and quash that warrant. You understand?"

"Yes sir." I said, and they took off up the block.

Holy shit, what a close one, but all together it made no sense. How do you stop someone, find out they have a warrant and not arrest them, based on "that's not what we're out here for today". The last time my name got ran and that same warrant came up, no questions asked, they took me in.

Over the next two months, I continued my little gig with Brad. Business kept me nice and tight with my heroin, but physically I was a mess. I was about 30 lbs. underweight, I picked up and smoked cigarette butts off of the ground, and I hadn't showered in over a month. When I decided my clothes were too ripe and musty for my own preference, I went into Value Village and stole jeans, shirts, and jackets. As for socks and hygiene supplies, I got those as the Union Gospel Mission's van came around.

I even saw Sarah a bit off and on when she'd come down after working Aurora, and we'd walk around the block for a while catching up, talking about the wacky couple of months up at Mark and Pam's.

In March, I spent most of that month running around with a few new groups of low level dealers. There were maybe eight or ten people out of the probably fifty dealers on the block that were not strung out. The rest of us supporting our habits would push dope throughout the day, but only so we could stay well, and damn near every one of us slept out of doors. A large number of these folx could be found along the back side of Macy's on Fourth Ave, bundled up in cardboard and disaster blankets from 11 p.m.to 7 a.m. Outside of that group, the rest would be scattered up by the Paramount Theatre, the on ramp by the convention center or back over to the Jungle under I-5.

My use had increased exponentially and Brad was in between connects, so I needed to learn to boost from the stores to come up with goods or money to stay well. Most of this new crew I was with were experts in retail theft. David, who helped me with that blanket early on, was the go to guy for bath and beauty supplies. Loco was the guy for high end clothing and hats. Allison was consistent at getting perfumes and such from Victoria's Secret. Everyone had an area of expertise. When people came down to the block with special requests for stolen goods in trade for cash or dope, these were the kind of people that got the work.

My thing became high end sunglasses. I'd get a decent outfit from the thrift shop, throw it on, carry an umbrella, and walk into one of the stores with designer shades available. I'd stand right there talking over the aisles with a store rep while I slid a pair of $400 Gucci glasses into the umbrella. I'd walk right out the door and get $50-$75 for them within ten minutes and 300 yards from where I stole them. That kind of cash could get me a small amount of dope to use and work with for a couple days if I played it right.

I stole most of what I ate in the last month and a half on the block. Whether it was from Walgreens or Bartell, I'd gotten caught a few times, tackled right outside the door, trespassed, and told not to come back. I'm not proud of any of it, but this is the nature of the person I was when I was addicted and strung out, and I was regularly criminalized for being addicted, homeless and hungry.

By April, the weather had started to warm up and it was a little easier to be sleeping outdoors. The downtown ambassador patrols had steadily been moving me on from my stoop in Post Alley, and I had started spending my nights under the monorail by Fifth and Westlake. During the day, I used to stash my bedroll behind a cardboard bailer in the loading dock for Ruth's Chris Steakhouse, and only took and used what I needed based on the weather at night.

Brad and I were pretty much done as far as business goes. His new connection didn't offer as good of a price, and given how much I was using it was a risk for him to float me anything in hopes of getting straight money back. I don't blame him; he had his own habit to look out for.

I was getting really desperate to stay well, so I even started flying a sign outside of Pacific Place some mornings just to get well so I could figure out the rest of the day's dope needs. I felt like my life was really coming to a close out here, and I was unsure as to what the end was going to look like.

Over the last couple of months while living on the streets downtown, I saw a dead body after a shooting at Third and Pine at 2 a.m. before the coroner hauled them off. I spent time with people who could not stop using dope despite living with HIV/AIDS, homelessness, and potentially spending the next five to ten years behind bars associated with crimes committed to score drugs. I've sat on loading docks with teens between 16 and 18 years old sticking needles into their already gangrenous or abscessed body tissue, simply because it's fucking hard to stop using. I have a scar through my eyebrow from having it split open in a street fight in the middle of Third Ave at 9 a.m. in front of the buses and commuters. I pissed in old pop bottles and shit in alleys because I was no longer allowed in the shops around the neighborhood to use their bathrooms.

In all of this I blame no one. Not even myself. I was doing the best I felt I could to find relief from some internal pain that started years earlier. I learned a long time ago that this way worked, but it wasn't sustainable, and I didn't want to admit that. But at the end of the day, I'm just like anyone else who doesn't want to suffer in this life.

Finally, the walls closed in. I got up under the monorail one morning to the bike patrols moving everybody along earlier than usual. As people congregated closer to Third Ave, the arrests began. Some of us watched as our friends and dealers got picked off and picked up one by one as they made their way up to the Blade. Within the course of twenty-four hours, the block went from jumping with the business and nonsense associated with trying to get right for the day, to a mess of dope-sick addicts wandering around like zombies hoping to come across someone still holding.

Benny had been one of the steady go to's for many of us that last month before the arrests. He sold a little bit of everything; sort of a one stop shop for us polysubstance users. He was staying up north on Aurora and as the sweeps started he immediately told everyone to call from a payphone and come to the Jack in the Box at 125th.

When Sarah came down to the Blade and found out the long anticipated sweep had started, she asked, "Do you know where we can get anything?"

"Yeah, let's get on the next E-Line, you got a cell phone?" I asked.

"Yep."

"Ok, dial this number." I said, and then she handed the phone over.

"Alright, let's pool what we have. He said he'll make it worth our while to come up there." I said, as I passed the phone back to Sarah.

Once we met Benny at the Jack in the Box and got high, Sarah went off to meet a client to get a little more cash to get us through the night. Since Benny was my hook up and she didn't know where else to go, she was going to put me on for helping her score.

When she returned, we called him expecting him to still be close.

"Nah man, I'm down here on the Blade, and then I'm heading south to Georgetown for the night. If you can get here by 10 p.m. I'll meet you, otherwise you gotta wait 'til tomorrow. I don't need anybody coming down to where I'm staying." he said.

"Cool we're on our way. Catching the bus now."

We got to Belltown and walked up to First Ave and Virginia St to meet him. Right after getting the dope, we walked over the vacant cobblestone stretch in Pike Place Market to the stairwell by Pike Brewery to crash for the night.

It was just short of midnight on April 23, 2015.

13

Release to the Community

The activities with the other veterans were helpful in breaking up the monotony of treatment programming and the regular jail schedule. It was nice to break off into a separate group and talk about where we had served, what our tours were like etc. Out of seven veterans, three of us were attending the mindfulness class on Saturdays.

People were completing the outpatient programming, moving on to work release, including Happy, and trustee spots were opening up. I regularly made myself available to help out with unit clean-up, and with Max vouching for me, I was given a position as a unit worker. The great part about this was that I got to spend time with the couple of individuals that were serious about staying clean, and with that I had a lot of time out of my cell while most other guys were in theirs. This allowed me to have more concentrated work-out routines, and access to the showers and phones when everybody else was locked down. Since I had so much rack out time, I spent less and less time out with the majority of the unit during the day. It was my first exercise in setting boundaries for my recovery. I was told I needed to change people, places and things; and this was a learning opportunity.

This was the same time that I would come across the book Dharma Punx by author and Buddhist teacher Noah Levine. The look of his tattooed hands on the cover in tandem with the title presented itself as something I could get into for the next few rack backs.

I dove into the book after dinner and was immediately pulled in. There was resonance for me with the music he got down with and some of the challenges he experienced in his earlier years. Reading on about how he started meditating in a correctional facility, and the search for freedom was coincidental. I had also arrived at the junction of combining traditional recovery processes like the twelve steps, with the spiritual practices of yoga and meditation.

Noah was laying out his experience and I began to understand how I could be responsible for my own freedom and happiness, without drugs or alcohol. I saw it possible that if I had done so much damage and endured suffering at the hands of my own actions, I must surely possess the ability to create peace and ease in my life as well.

I finished the book by the next afternoon, and when I returned it to the shelf, there was Essential Writings, a book by Thich Nhat Hanh; more Buddhism. Looking back now, the more I believed that I was onto something and it was working for me, the more the path of recovery was presenting itself, day after day.

Through this book, I started to learn to practice gratitude with my current living situation. I learned to be grateful for the running water and toilet I had in my cell. Some might find this type of practice a little outrageous, but towards the end of my run on the streets, nobody was letting me in anywhere to use a public restroom or wash my hands. I had been trespassed in most of the downtown shopping stores and/or security followed me wherever I went once inside. When I got up in the mornings, I had to piss in an alley and scrounge enough change to buy a black drip coffee to gain access to a restroom, just to take a shit. I now had a steady roof over my head for the first time in months.

I also began to check in on what was working for me in my physical body, and even learned to embrace some discomfort. Understanding that I could be grateful for not having a headache, things of that nature. Much of the previous years had been spent with no regard for my physical welfare, beating up on my mind and body, always trying to get away from the slightest dis-ease or unpleasant sensations. Being present and appreciative for my current situation wasn't exactly an experience I was willing to share with the other guys; but it really changed the way I felt about my personal circumstances. I learned suffering and happiness were created by my relationship to experience, and not by the experience itself.

I had a legit daily practice going on in there, a solid recovery foundation; and I had no idea just how much security I was establishing towards keeping my recovery moving upon my release from jail.

As the next few weeks rolled on, I completed the outpatient programming but spots at work release were pretty backed up, so it didn't look like I would be getting out as quickly as I thought. My dad's health was in steady decline, and it was seeming my mom would have to put him in a care facility within the next month or two. I was feeling overwhelmed with needing to get down to Cali to see him, spend time with my daughter, and really just figuring out how to stay dope free in the community. I was still hitting the twelve step meetings, and I kept hearing about the inventory and amends process. With that, there was all this stuff coming up about forgiveness and compassion with the spiritual and Buddhist practices, and I knew I had much work ahead of me.

There were a few people in the unit with me that I had some difficult experiences with on the street. One guy in particular had ripped me off on some black, gave me some shit with coffee mixed in it; total garbage. The last interaction with him ended with me threatening him and holding him up against a wall until the police rolled up on us.

By now I was feeling pretty bad about that whole thing. There were a lot of folx to have compassion for, but here was one guy I really needed to straighten things out with. I needed to start forgiving myself and others. Yeah he ripped me off, but if I was intent on leaving that way of life behind, I needed to start here and now. After all he was a suffering addict, just like me.

I caught him walking laps around the yard one evening and said, "Hey, can I talk to you for a minute?"

"Yeah I guess." he got standoffish and looked concerned.

"Look man, I said some things to you last time I saw you out there. I was sick and upset about that dope deal, and I was being a real asshole and I threatened you. I'd like to apologize for my part in that whole thing and ask for your forgiveness.

He looked completely baffled, "Are you serious?" he asked. "Hey, I appreciate it, but I'm the one who needs to be apologizing. I ripped you and a lot of other people off."

"Well honestly, don't worry about it. You won't find me back out there. I want to be done with all of this, and I thought this would be a good place to start."

"For sure, thanks." he said. "Let me know if I can do anything."

"Yeah, thanks as well; we're good though." I said.

Damn. That felt pretty fucking good. In most cases that would be some risky shit, especially in this environment, but hey, it landed pretty well. So this is what freedom feels like?

I would go on to learn a lot about forgiveness while in jail and moving forward in becoming a more skillful human. The practice of forgiveness for myself and others has illuminated the darkest moments of my life in making the transition from addiction to recovery. To forgive is to take a radical approach and attempt to cause less harm; it's an act of mercy for myself and those around me. Therefore, acceptance is not the answer to my problems, forgiveness is. To forgive is to let go; letting go of the hopes of a better past, letting go of resentment, letting go of self-hatred. And to let go is to accept the world and conditions as they are, allowing us to cultivate the ability to move forward with an open and compassionate heart.

On the following Friday, one of the veterans program case workers came to see me and asked, "Didn't you already complete the treatment portion? What are you still doing here?"

"Yeah I did, but work release is backed up for another thirty days or so; I have to wait for spots to free up."

"Would you be willing to go to a veteran's shelter if it were available?" she asked.

"Absolutely, anywhere. I just want to see my daughter and maybe take a trip to visit my parents ASAP."

"I'll call your drug court case manager and ask if they'll cut you loose if we can confirm an opening." she said.

"That sounds great, I'd really appreciate it."

A few hours later, my outpatient programming counselor came into the unit and called me in from the yard.

"Well, are you ready to get out and work your recovery?" he asked.

"Shit yeah, why?" I asked, taken completely off guard.

"Your case manager approved the bed at the Salvation Army shelter. You're out Monday morning."

Man, I was ecstatic! Monday morning? Two days and a wake up and I'm outta here.

Monday August 31st at 5:30 a.m. I was transported back to Seattle and released to drug court orientation; that little intake I skipped out on months earlier. As a reminder of the filthy lifestyle I lived in active heroin addiction, I had to wear the clothes that were in my property at release. The musty smell of the shirt and pants that I had worn for over a month without washing was completely embarrassing; and to make things worse they had festered in a big zip lock property bag for the last four months. Nothing like putting that shit back on to truly remind me of where my addiction had taken me.

Both Brian and I got released the same day; sat through the drug court program overview, expectations, and did assessments with case managers. Sometime after 11:30 a.m. I was out the door of the courthouse again and on Third Ave. I remember the first feeling that washed over me; this place. The last time I came out of jail onto this street, I hadn't had any dope in almost two weeks, yet was loaded again within an hour.

I was asking myself, "What's different this time Joe?"

I now had supports on the outside. I had a veteran's case manager already expecting me to make contact about the shelter process for the afternoon, and I was told I could always knock on the drug court door and ask for help.

The tricky thing was that the shelter bed was not exactly an ideal model for most drug court participants, since many go to work release and have little free time on their hands while they adjust to life in the community. And to top it off, drug court is aware that relapse may be part of the process to establishing recovery and it makes room for the challenges of reentering the community, but some of the other guys I got released with saw this as an opportunity to get loaded without increased treatment expectations for a week or two. I also had a book of bus tickets from drug court, with a value of about $10, equivalent to a quick hit of dope.

The problem with all of that thinking for me was "If I pick up, will I actually be able to stop again?" I had more than 90 days of clean time, why throw it away because I could get away with it? I believed if I don't do this recovery thing now, I'll never do it. The lying and stealing will begin and I'll be all over trying to relieve my shame and guilt. This is the best fighting chance if one has ever been available to me.

I did what was suggested in treatment, the next right thing, and turned and headed south to the VA office to meet my case manager.

The area around the Lazarus Day Center was Pioneer Square's hot spot for crack users. I watched the cravings come to the surface as I made my way to the door, realizing I don't have to act on the feeling; that it would actually pass if I just let it. I walked in, signed some paperwork, was given a brand new backpack that I would use for my drug court info and treatment assignments, and received my check in time for the Salvation Army Center. I quickly left the area and made my way over to the Booth Center.

I was an hour early when I arrived at the entrance to the shelter center. I was told in TRP to change my people, places and things if I wanted to see results and truly stop getting loaded, so sitting here waiting rather than uptown or around the courthouse was aligning me with these new possibilities; even though it was uncomfortable; and that was a good thing.

For the first time in my life I was sitting with discomfort, with the unknown. At that moment, I had what is known as a beginner's mind. I knew very little about what it takes to be someone in recovery, and I was ok with being with my new situation as it was unfolding, riding out those old urges to do what I used to when I got released. But this wasn't the same, regardless if it shared characteristics of all my previous releases, this was a brand new experience if I would just let it be. I no longer needed to act from my old habit patterns. This time could be rooted in what my past experiences had shown me, that I'm powerless over drugs and alcohol, and many other things. But knowing that I couldn't use drugs and alcohol out here in this moment was big; knowing that I didn't need to, and feeling that I didn't want to. This was the first time I would respond with wisdom rather than delusion.

I got checked in, assigned a bunk, and was given some fresh clothes and shower gear. There was a phone that was available for free calls, and I got a hold of Rachael so I could plan to see Ione. Simultaneously, I started thinking about how I should find out where the nearest twelve step meetings are and attend one before I do anything, but I really needed to see and hold my daughter.

Rachael answered and said she would help us get together for a couple of hours if I could make my way south.

"Ok, I'll be catching the next bus down there to the transit center in about twenty min, should be there in forty-five." I said.

I grabbed my bag and ran out the door to the closest bus stop. It was 5:30 p.m. rush hour and the bus schedules were way off with traffic. I ended up waiting for twenty minutes before my bus arrived. At this rate I would be an additional twenty-five minutes, and without my own cell phone for another day or two I had no way to let them know.

I hadn't been out a full day and was already making it like business as usual for her and my kid; telling them I'm going to be somewhere and then not being there. Great start this is turning out to be.

When the bus pulled into the transit center, I could see the blue Volkswagen Jetta sitting there with my daughter climbing around in it.

Ok, they're still here; well that's good news. I ran up to the car, and right away I started explaining myself, why I was late and what happened with the buses. Rachael wasn't trying to hear any of it, not after the months leading up to that last arrest. All the excuses, all the lies, all the betrayal. Nope.

"Just get in the car." she said with frustration.

Surprisingly I chose to just hear what she said and not engage back in anger. And for the most part it went on to be a good evening; it felt incredible to actually hold my daughter, free from the idea that I would have to leave her again at the pull of my addiction and expense of my relationship with her.

The benefit of staying at the Booth Center was that I didn't have to report back to the shelter until midnight, at the latest. I didn't have an outpatient treatment agency intake for another week and a half, so I had time to catch up with my kid and begin attending support meetings, establishing some kind of recovery routine. That first night out of custody I rolled back north on public transit about 10 p.m. feeling all sorts of emotions and sensory experiences I had dumbed down for so long. I had a strong, overwhelming sense of excitement about the road ahead, like actually able to think about living a life free from addiction. I needed to start living a life in recovery, and that was going to require new, healthy habits and engagement with people doing this thing in the community.

The next morning I got up and headed over to the drug court office. I felt one day in the community without a meeting and establishing new supports was already playing with fire. I was flipping through the local AA meeting book when I found "Cherry Fellowship Hall."

I was sitting with my case manager, Martin, and I asked, "Can you look up what bus will take me up to this address?"

He said, "Oh that place? The number three bus picks up right on the side of the courthouse and brings you almost to the doorstep of the hall. That bus route runs about every ten minutes, and they have about three or four meetings there a day."

"Great, thanks!" I said.

I showed up to Cherry Hall about fifteen minutes before the meeting ended. I was antsy about needing some contacts before I left there for the day, so when the chairperson asked if there were any burning desires, I piped up.

"Hey I'm Joe, I'm an addict/alcoholic and I just got out of jail yesterday morning. I have a little over 100 days and I'm grateful to be at a meeting outside of custody. I don't know anyone here but I know I need to be here, plus the judge said it would be a good idea."

I got some chuckles about the judge comment and a few "thanks for sharing", and my meeting book filled up with phone numbers to call. The guy that was chairing came up and introduced himself to me, and offered to have me call and check in with him regularly. Sam encouraged me to come to the hall on Wednesday nights for a beginner's meeting, and I told him I'd see him there.

Over the next week I checked in with Sam on and off, stopped by the court, and spent time with my daughter. I would take her to the park while her mom made small batches of kale chips at a friend's kitchen in Pioneer Square.

I got started on my IOP treatment and UA's about two and a half weeks after my release from TRP. This was really good; it added CBT, counselor one on one's, group sessions and two random UA's per week. I really wasn't motivated by just the court or the time hanging over my head. I was truly enjoying getting to know myself and navigating my day to day with the ability to appreciate my overall freedom, not just from jail but from the substances and behaviors that weighed me down for the last fifteen years.

Once I began IOP I got used to a tight schedule. I would get up in the morning at the Booth Center, lift weights or practice yoga outside in the courtyard or at the YMCA, come back, eat and shower, then bus it up to Therapeutic Health Services where I did my treatment; and that was three days per week. Once I got out of treatment for the day, I would call and check in on my parents while walking back the thirty minutes to the Booth Center. After lunch, I would use the prayer/dedication room at the shelter to practice my meditation in the afternoons, then head out to catch up with my kid.

My father wasn't doing well, and the amount of care he required was increasing. My mom was sorting things out to get him into a veteran care facility in SoCal. His dementia had progressed so badly that he lacked balance and his memory and state of awareness was all over the place. Compounded with my mother's back pain and restless states, this was all a combination bound for disaster if she were to try to keep him at home. He had already had an incident earlier in the year where he wandered out of the house in the middle of the night, fell and hit his head on a curb. All of this decline was going on as I had been selfishly calling my mother for money for my heroin addiction. I couldn't even put my ill father before my addiction when I was out there; I had been a self-centered mess. I knew my dad wasn't doing well, so I also continued my use as a way to escape the reality that his health was worsening and I might be dead before him, or that he might pass on while I'm in jail or prison.

Outside of the health issues with my parents, things were getting progressively better in other areas of my personal life. The no-contact order with Rachael was lifted due to my compliance with drug court, and I was hitting about five meetings a week on top of my IOP sessions, making new, healthy friends in the recovery rooms.

One of the Wednesdays there was a man there, about twenty years older than me, and he expressed all the same difficulties with his family relationships due to his addiction that I had in mine. The arguments, lost jobs, getting out of the car and not coming back for a week; all of the cries of "I promise I won't do it again", only to do it again. Having to explain why the paycheck is gone two days after payday, but the rent didn't get handled. In much of it, it appeared that he and I used drugs and harmed our personal relationships in similar ways.

When the meeting was over, Sam came up to me and said, "You could ask Paul to be your sponsor. I was thinking his story might sound familiar?"

"Yeah, it really did. All of it." I said.

"Do you want me to introduce you guys?" he asked.

"Yes, definitely."

Paul and I got to talking, he asked some questions about my recovery up to this point, what substances I had been into, and a little about my court and family situation.

"I'll meet you back here next Wednesday, at the eatery across the street one hour before the meeting. I'd like you to read the Foreword to the First Edition, Bill's Story, and The Doctor's

Opinion. Highlight everything that resonates, and make notes of anything you don't agree with. We'll go from there. Sound good?"

"You got it, sounds great. Thank you." I said.

Paul and I would continue to meet like that every Wednesday for the next six months. He was willing to work as fast and as hard as I was, yet he was thorough. He was versed in the history of the program, which gave some great context to the events and timelines around when the book was being written, and how the program continued to unfold throughout the 20th century. He was also very supportive of my meditation and yoga practices and how those improved the foundation and quality of my recovery. In the midst of the twelve step process, I was burning through works by individuals who have written on addiction, recovery, meditation and spirituality. "Autobiography of a Yogi" by Paramahansa Yogananda was one of the first yoga reads and essential eye openers of devotion to spiritual awakening that was speaking to me in a way that expanded upon my existing recovery work.

It was time to take a trip down to see my dad. I had done a lot of work around my fears inventory, and I needed to be proactive in facing the fear of losing my father. I also needed him to see me in recovery before he passed. I wanted to look him in the eyes and tell him I was sorry for the way I lived, whether he could understand or comprehend made no difference to me. I just didn't want him to pass on and never have gotten to be sober and present with his condition. Rachael, Ione and I got the tickets and went down to Cali for a four day visit. When we got off the plane, my mom picked us up and we went straight to the care facility to see him.

This was one of the most difficult times of my early recovery; accepting the one person I've known to be my hero, my unconditional support, relegated to a wheelchair and being spoon fed. This is what my addiction had done to my understanding; it had me still clinging to the "glory days". The days of looking up to his work and character, those evenings when he got off of work and we would go golfing, and our other past times together. It wouldn't allow me to begin to accept the impermanence of life itself, and I had sought through substances (towards the end of my using) to hold onto the happier memories I had with my father.

Regardless of the discomfort of this reality, he still lit up when he saw me. He looked tired, and worn out and didn't resemble the man I spent so much time with back in 2010. He looked like he aged twenty years since I last saw him. The days were hard and sad for him, in my opinion. Most of them were spent in some state of belief that he was still fixing machines, out on location, running with the guys. It was unbearable to watch him think he dropped a machine part or tool and try to lean forward out of his wheelchair to pick up something that wasn't really there. Any form of conversation we engaged in was always relative to his work or people from the past. My experience with my dad and dementia was like watching someone travel back through time in their life history, heading in reverse back to their younger years, and when he finally reached his beginning, it all ends. The worse the dementia progressed, the further back his memory lapsed and he thought and acted like he was existing in a different time and place; because with the illness, he was.

And I learned I could face it all; the way he looked and how he responded, his entire condition, because I actually had the emotional capability to fucking cry about the impending loss of my father, as well as the beauty of being here with him sober. Feeling it once and for all, the fleeting nature of life itself.

By the second day I was emotionally exhausted, and felt disconnected from my practice. It was too difficult for me to sit in meditation with the amount of sadness, grief and anxiety I felt. I was just being aware enough to say "I can't do this, it's too unpleasant and too challenging, right now in this moment". With all that going on internally, I felt like taking a trip to the ocean, and I remembered some of the final pages of Autobiography of a Yogi, and the practice Yogananda was doing at the Encinitas hermitage, which was only an hour and half drive from Hemet where my mom lived. We decided it would be a good way to decompress to make the short pilgrimage to the Self Realization Meditation Fellowship, and spend the day walking the same grounds as Paramahansa had some seventy years earlier.

To me this was an incredible opportunity. This again was one of the many synchronicities of vibrating on higher consciousness in recovery, being open to receive the benefits of seeking awakening and understanding. The grounds were beautiful, and the meditation gardens and koi ponds brought an instant tranquility and calm over all the emotional upheaval I was experiencing. Even Ione at four years old was willing to sit and acknowledge the captivating flowers and other foliage.

I returned to Seattle, back to my drug court and recovery programs, and was digging further into my yoga practice. I was attending asana classes as often as possible, and after four months at the veteran's shelter, I was welcomed to move in at Rachael's mother's house with her and Ione. I was also gaining traction in many other areas of my life. Brad, a good friend from the twelve step rooms since day one, had given me some part time work doing apartment clean outs and landscaping, and compensated me more than fairly for my time and energy; and I felt valued and my self-worth gradually increased.

I found a local yoga studio that was offering Y12SR classes (Yoga of 12 Step Recovery). This practice is a wonderful blend of the twelve step philosophy and physical practice of yoga asana, skillfully integrated by Nikki Myers.

In my mind this was addressing more of the discomforts that were associated with an aging body, but even more so, the ravaging effect of what drugs, alcohol and the lifestyle had done to my physical state. It was becoming increasingly difficult to go in and out of some recovery meetings, watching the overconsumption of sweets, coffee and cigarettes while these folks told others how to recover. All I could think about were the days toward the end of my time on the streets and how terrible my diet had been. It consisted of high sugar foods, alcohol, narcotics and nicotine and practically no intake of water. After all of the addictions and four months of a high pork diet at the shelter and being grateful for whatever food was on my plate, I had some detoxification to do.

A personal recovery program that does not address our physical wellbeing, relationships to food and how our addiction manifests in other areas of our lives is missing the mark all-together. I believed I ought to explore my relationship to all things that I put into my body on a daily basis.

For me, yoga and the culture around the practices encouraged more mindful awareness of what I was eating and how I was eating, in terms of non-harming of living creatures etc. and I went vegan. This wasn't the first time I was totally meat-free, but this had purpose and intention behind it. I will say the rigidity of being vegan in early recovery was helping my renouncing of substances and abstinence in other harmful behaviors, but ultimately I would go in and out of veganism. I focused on being mostly plant based; adding small amounts of fish in my diet, but never reverting back to red meat, or poultry. I still do a lot of experimenting to find out just how good I can feel physically, and how to obtain optimal performance in mind and body. With that said, time and time again it has served me well to look closely at and evaluate what I'm filling this body, head and heart up with; whether it is food, beverage or bringing awareness to my consumption of news and media.

As for deepening my yoga asana practice, I sought to do a teacher training. I found an evening activity with a local student of B.K.S. Iyengar, where he offered an "Introduction to Teacher Training". I attended it, and was drawn in right away. The only catch was the 200 hour level certification was thousands of dollars; absolutely top of the line training, but I didn't have the money for it.

A week later, I was attending an orientation at a local agency in Seattle, the Recovery Café, that drug court staff suggested I check out as another community and recovery resource.

It's an amazing concept, as they are a drop in style center where folx in recovery from anything can go and be in a safe and supportive environment. There are meetings, support circles, meals, coffee, peer support/recovery coaching, and I was able to fulfill my community service hours there. There were art and writing classes; but what really caught my attention were the yoga classes, as well as a free yoga teacher training.

This can't be correct, I thought, so I asked the operations manager about it.

"No, for real. We have a free certification program. 200 hour level training." he said.

"What do I have to do to get started?" I asked.

"Come in on a Wednesday and talk to John. Older gentleman, he runs the yoga program."

I came back the next available Wednesday and walked in, introducing myself to the only older guy in the room. He had to be in his 60's.

John said, "If you're interested, I recommend you attend a few of the classes to begin with, then if you still want to do it, it's just $7 for the training manual and you'll need to obtain the required books for the program, but we'd be happy to have you. Work on it at your own pace too."

John owned a studio not too far up the road, and spent his days running the studio and teaching yoga asana and the curriculum at the café. He had years of teaching experience and personal practice. The program offered all of the fixings of other yoga trainings like anatomy and sutra study, classes most days, chant, and had writing and teaching assignments. I was all over this opportunity and got my materials right away.

Over the next couple of months I was still attending IOP with Max, Happy, and Brian, hanging out with them from time to time; and Rachael and I had a kale chip business moving in a direction that seemed like we might actually need to get a license and start selling our products on a larger scale.

It was saddening to watch the level of engagement in drug court decline as some of the familiar faces disengaged from the program. Sort of this one foot in the door of the program and the other in the old lifestyle. Some of the people from TRP started to voluntarily terminate or go on warrant, some would come to the group loaded, or deal dope right outside the treatment agency. Some of them overdosed and died. Yet some were completing the program too, getting their felonies dismissed and maintaining their recovery.

Staff in charge of the incarcerated veterans program reached out to me about my progress after being released from the RJC jail, and wanted me to come share my story to a county council member and another guy from the bureau of prisons. They wanted to talk about my participation in the vets program and how it had been supporting me, as well as my experiences with drug court, addiction, recovery, the reentry process, and the kale chip business. Lastly, they asked if the local news agency could do a story on me.

I started thinking about what I was learning in terms of how sharing my story in the rooms was supposed to be helpful to others, and maybe this was another way to reach people who had friends or family living with substance use disorder and it could inspire some hope by shedding light on local support programs. So in the spirit of service work I said yes; and the idea was to have the news piece released on Veteran's Day 2016, still some months away.

Along the way of gathering the footage and info for this, the kale business really got off the ground. We managed to get into farmers markets and a handful of stores; all legit with a business license and a certified kitchen we started renting down by the stadiums.

Getting the kale thing moving was surreal. It was a seemingly unattainable business idea from a couple years earlier that Rachael kept alive while I was doing my dirt and spent those few months in jail. Selling kale at the markets was like selling dope on the streets for me. I had a product that people liked, they came to see me, gave me their cash, and walked away with a smile on their face.

Many folx would come back week after week and tell me how much they loved the chips. People were blown away by the flavors and business model. After years of working farmers markets for other growers, it was easy to source local and organic produce and have awesome relationships within that community. This became yet another place where I got plugged in; I had support and people that believed in me, and didn't seem to care about my story and how big of a selfish asshole I had been. Maybe they did care about my past and the things I did, but they were not about to measure me by the things I had done to hold me back from where I was headed.

I could point to the farmer across the way from us and say, "Yeah that's where the kale comes from. We buy it, season and dehydrate it, then bring it back to the market on our table a few days later like this."

Customers would say, "Wow that's incredible, they're so addictive!"

I don't ever recall personally using the word "addictive" to describe food, but that's what we were told. Kind of a funny turn of events.

When I got released from jail, I realized how I had potentially destroyed my reputation based on the financial decisions I made with the farm invoices to support my drug use. I felt like the shame I lived with around those actions could have been enough to send me back out to use based on what I knew about resentments, so I took matters into my own hands.

I was told this was unwise or that maybe I wasn't ready to hear what some people may have had to say about my choices and how it affected them, but I had to take action. I went ahead and got my old email list from the produce wholesaling, and composed an email stating my poor choices, how it unfolded, and touched on that I had been incarcerated relating to my substance use. I was here to own my part, willing to make things right, and asked how I could do so.

Every email response I received was not only encouraging, but I also found out how many people I was already connected to that were either in recovery or knew someone that had similar struggles. Some even asked if there was anything they could do to be supportive, or offered to get together and hit a meeting.

I realize that this isn't the case in amends for every person in recovery, but my ability to create and stay connected to a supportive community was dependent on taking this action. This one couldn't wait; I was about to be back in the Seattle food scene trying to make a living and I needed to unpack my wrong-doings and ask for forgiveness.

The local entrepreneurial scene became yet another place where I found immense support; there were free or low cost business growing opportunities; and minority, women or veteran owned business classes with some small loans available.

Resources, accessibility, and community; that's how progress was possible for me, in multiple areas. These things don't exist in a vacuum, they travel together or they don't work. The other thing is that none of these opportunities or resources were available without structure and accountability. I lacked those in my personal life based on my history with substances, and only chaos existed. Drug court had been providing structure and a container for me to become accountable and responsible in my life. With those qualities, I found it possible to wrap my head around running a business.

Then tragedy struck again. Two days after Christmas, I was driving with my daughter and I took a call from my cousin back in Massachusetts.

"We lost another one Joe."

Not yet phased I asked, "Well, now who?"

"Will." he said; and we both fell silent for a moment.

Chris knew how far back he and I went. He knew this was bigger than Pete and Jeff.

I actually had a few minutes to talk with Chris about this one, and he went on to say that he had taken his own life. It didn't make it any easier, but since I wasn't using drugs anymore, I felt a shift in my usual response.

Key word here is "response". I had been doing meditations on compassion and equanimity, and I was immediately able to access a place of warmth and spaciousness around this news. It didn't need to be about how to not feel this pain in this moment. I was actually turning towards the hurt I felt, and this was no longer about me. This was around someone else's suffering, someone I considered like a brother since grade school. I began to empathize with the place he must have been in to make that decision. He had beautiful kids, a big family; but something was just too painful, too challenging. And shit, didn't I barely make it out of a place like that not so long ago?

It was at this moment that I realized I would not have to suffer about this; I didn't need to meet this loss with hatred. I wanted to work with and understand this loss the best that I could. I spent the following two weeks working with a practice of gratitude for our friendship, the practice of loving-kindness for his family; one member at time, experiencing freedom from suffering around his loss, and being at ease. I also opened up and cried to my family about his passing, and didn't need to move away from vulnerability or reality through substances. This is what freedom is. Freedom from drugs was freedom to feel, experience, and appreciate life and death, in the fullest way possible.

As difficult as this death was, I was feeling assured I could deal with adversities in my life without using drugs. I was able to discuss this in my treatment groups, and I also got a chance to work with my counselor about writing how his death felt to me.

I had now reached Phase Three of the drug court program, and was expected to attend an Empowerment Class, facilitated by the housing case manager, Shannon.

Shannon has an astonishing ability to take challenging pieces of information with often difficult individuals, break them down piecemeal and turn them into teachable moments for everyone with a wide range of topics relevant to personal progress and accountability.

He uses a 100 minute class to decipher what empowerment is and what it is not. Participants come away with an understanding that the survival skills of life in addiction or enslavement to our behaviors have translatable values that we can take into our lives in recovery and beyond. He covers areas of our life that tend to suffer or become strained when one is addicted, and how our personal empowerment can help repair and sustain from then on.

At that point in the program, the individual is most likely to be stable in their recovery, in action or maintenance in the stages of change. They may be working on gaining or maintaining employment; with disengagement from illegal activity and actively building supportive community; yet getting to this point requires great effort, energy and self-awareness.

I've found this to be true of any process of recovery; they are paths and/or programs for people that want them, not people that need them. There is much to be gained and much more to lose, depending on how successfully we identify who our supportive community is, and our ability to tap into that and withdraw ourselves from the old subcultures of our addiction. Many people walk into the rooms of recovery and diagnose themselves right out on a basis of "this won't work for me"; I know because I did it in the last few years of my addiction. Same thing happens in diversion programs/therapeutic courts. A particular challenge

in administering these models is one must take into consideration the war on drugs and how it affects communities of color;
and the historical role that the criminal legal system has played in
the life of a drug addict over the years. How do certain community members trust a system that has typically failed to uphold
justice and/or create equity for certain populations for centuries?

Furthermore, I believe from experience that some of us have a
difficult time accepting help, because we don't recognize it in the
form it takes when it shows up. For example, major crimes task
force arrested me and started the process of my gaining access to
the drug court program, and I got separated from narcotics, and
became willing to accept it as something bigger working in my
life. But surely not at first. It's difficult to believe that being dope-
sick in custody is somehow helpful, and in most cases it isn't.

I don't blindly agree with the legal system and how it interacts
with addicted populations, but would I have stopped without
that legal intervention? I know I wanted help, but I sure wasn't
happy about the way it showed up that morning, in the form
of an arrest and a week of dope sickness in custody. I wanted a
soft landing, maybe some muscle relaxers, marijuana and a TV
marathon while I withdrew from heroin, but I burnt up those
opportunities in my addiction. And realistically, I'd had enough,
but just didn't know how to stop using. An arrest and jail started
the process of getting me stopped, drug court obligations, recovery programs and community helped me to stay stopped. Recovery is hard work, and asked me to do a lot of things, some of them
uncomfortable, but nothing quite as uncomfortable as the rep-
tilian shit I had to do to get dope every day. Drug court expected

me to show up for my recovery barely one-third of how my addiction asked me to show up.

The truth is I did get a soft landing though. I had been arrested seven times altogether in two years and never once did I fear for my life when faced with police. I will say that I've had rough encounters with law enforcement, having been shoved around with guns drawn on me, but the whole system itself favors white people like me in safely exiting it because it's set up to. I really had no record, no prior interactions with law enforcement just on the basis of being white and privileged, hardly suspected of any wrongdoing or coming off as threatening even as I sold heroin in the community and had been a perpetrator of domestic violence; that stuff my father told me was a Black and brown people issue. George Floyd was given a death sentence, murdered by police for suspicion of using a counterfeit bill to buy smokes. Many people have degraded and stigmatized him based on his criminal history, which reflect all of the very crimes and charges I have endured and survived with law enforcement without ever fearing for my life. Breonna Taylor was murdered by police on a no-knock drug raid warrant; yet years earlier I had been told by police Pete and I were being watched, and a raid never occurred. Though he died on the stretcher, police apparently didn't feel the need to barge in, prepared to gun us down that morning. Simply put, white cops gunning down white drug dealers wouldn't have made for good headlines in the local news. I stood before white judges as a white man, went to treatment and primarily had white counselors, surrounded by an overwhelming amount of white peers. I saw white people recovering and getting jobs in the treatment field after having been an addict, showing me that it was extremely difficult to be stripped of white privilege, even though I had been hung up on drugs and alcohol for fifteen years.

It began dawning on me that because of the criminalization of Black, Indigenous, People of Color (BIPOC) through the war on drugs, many other community members didn't get the opportunity I did because of the disadvantage of previous convictions due to drug policies meant to put BlPOC behind bars for decades. Non-white interactions with the system are often rooted in lengthy sentences instead of treatment, and the stories frequently seen in the mainstream media and majority accessible books by authors are about white men and women recovering, just like this one; showing us reintegrating to a healthy community.

The most prevalent programs meant to help folx recover were created by white men before the civil rights movement, and are dominated with white membership. Some already ostracize its members and limit their involvement in the group on the basis of taking medications, so other deep rooted racial biases are surely always at work. Most recovery programs (and to be very clear this is not just restricted to twelve step) and their members boast of everyone being equal in the rooms and stand behind hard lined tradition to say there is no opinion on outside issues, relegating groups to "colorblindness", and discounting the hardships and oppression BIPOC members endured prior to recovery, as well as the truth of their experience when the meeting is over and they walk out the door into all the "isms" in American culture. We cannot go on thinking there is anti-racism, anti-sexism work and so forth to do or programs to be re-evaluated for equity and success in every other facet of our society, minus recovery programs, resting on it being solely up to the individual to work an honest and thorough program. That is simply not good enough and programs ought to be willing to make statements and comb through any long-standing principles to address race and gender inequities and exclusion at the group level and beyond. True service and carrying the message to those that still suffer should be courageous and thorough enough to understand that just because we are addicts or alcoholics, the starting points and access to care and social constructs are not the same. Looking at one's part in things loses its value when we do inventory work that stops short of scratching the surface on larger causes and conditions like patriarchy and misogyny, intolerance towards the LGBTQ community and one's role in white supremacy and how it harms others. All of these are at work in our society and manifest in the realms of treatment, recovery and advocacy; often creating predatory and unsafe conditions to navigate for those seeking help. Getting down and undoing those injurious, deep-seated core beliefs in ourselves and our recovery programs is the true growth in understanding and effectiveness towards healing and recovery for all beings. Without exception, this work must extend to include close examination of our yoga and meditation practitioner communities; these other practices utilized for gaining insight and freedom from suffering around the human condition. These spiritual communities can easily become whitewashed beacons for the privileged with costly membership fees and lengthy, exotic retreats offering glorious meals and amenities; having been products of cultural appropriation here in the west and further limiting diverse participation and facilitators.

In the months leading up to my completing drug court, the steady decline of my father had really taken its toll on my mother. Her long drives to see my dad in the care facility combined with her back pain, stress, anxiety and depression made things increasingly difficult. She was heavily medicated on opiates, and eventually had an overdose.

I couldn't believe it. Here I am in drug court, for heroin of all things, and my mother is overdosing on prescription painkillers while my dad is on his way out. It started to feel like I might lose her first, followed by him. Was it worth getting upset at my mom? No, because I totally understood it. I knew why and how it happened; anticipatory grief was mounting and she needed to know I understood that pain and that I was willing to show up and support her.

I flew down and we decided to complete a power of attorney to me for her, in case anything further happened. I also took a trip to her prescriber with her while I was in town.

I can't explain the frustration of having to feel more adequately educated through my lived experience than a medical doctor in the nature of addiction and narcotics; especially while he's trying to justify prescribing your loved one more opiates shortly after an overdose. This would go on to become one of my first experiences battling a system that knowingly and unknowingly destroys lives, rather than help them. I implored this man to find another path forward for her pain management. And no, it's not my life to decide, but opiates and how they affected my mother were nothing new, and I sure wasn't letting this fly under the guise of being prescribed medication. Overdose had already taken too much from me, and I sure couldn't stand to lose my mother to one. I went on to be very candid with the doctor about my own struggle with opiate addiction and that I needed his support in understanding the impact opiates already had on my life and upbringing.

The last couple of months in the drug court program I was expected to meet in an aftercare group once a week, and see my chemical dependency counselor once a month. I went down to one random UA each week and attended sober support meetings, but for the most part, I just worked my food business at markets and my recovery program. On Tuesdays I sold the kale chips at a farmers market across from the superior courthouse, and occasionally when I had my hearings, I would have to be relieved from the stand to run up and get in front of the judge for five minutes to be seen, and given my phase promotion orders.

I graduated Drug Diversion Court sanction-free in just over twelve months, on September 14th, 2016, and the training wheels were off.

I had some of my peers ask, "What should I do when I complete drug court?" or any other program for that matter. My answer is always the same; all of the shit you were doing besides going to hearings and pissing in a cup and so on. If you went to meetings, continue to go to meetings; if you had a mental health counselor, stay engaged with them. Also, now is not the time to see what our old friends are up to. Find out if we have reservations about staying clean and share them with people in the recovery community. Chances are a sponsor or peer has good suggestions or insight.

Some months before graduation I was asked to take over as meeting secretary at a Back to Basics twelve step group. I still had that service position when I completed drug court, so naturally I knew where I needed to be in the evening on the day I graduated; right up in front of that room reading the preamble before turning it over to the chair. I recall thinking early on that my world would get smaller in sobriety; I was wrong. Since entering recovery my world had gotten so much bigger. Remember Nate, the building manager from the trap house in Queen Anne? Yep, he was in recovery and one of my first friends in the rooms. He's the one that asked me to take over the service position when his family member fell ill.

If completing an inpatient stay or program breaks up our new found recovery routine, we build our new routine in life around our meetings and time spent with our recovery practices and community, not the other way around.

The thing I know now is that the process of maintaining recovery can be daunting or overwhelming when seen through a similar lens into how difficult it was to maintain whatever chaos we tried to manage in our addiction. As the months went on and I obtained more time abstinent, I started to see things as a little more black and white. Got spare time? I go to a meeting or call someone in recovery until I can fill the new void with some other fruitful activity. Pissed off at something? I can practice gratitude, forgiveness, write inventory or practice mindfulness to get into the somatic experience of emotions rather than over identifying with them in my mind; watching the minute to minute arising and passing of physiological and worldly conditions.

I don't always remember in the moment, but I've found it useful when life is challenging to pause and ask "What would the best version of myself do right now?" And oftentimes I remember just after the not so helpful version of myself jumps out and reacts. I've come to understand that my first thought is usually unskillful, maybe a bit selfish or self-centered. I can still do the next right thing if I practice arriving here in this moment with an intention to cease reacting from my old habit patterns; responding with non-judgement and kindness, continuing along a pathway of positive change for myself and the those around me.

14

On Life's Terms

Less than a month after drug court graduation, I completed my 200 hour yoga teacher training in October with John at the Recovery Cafe. I had been engaged in a steady morning asana practice for the last seven or eight months and about thirty minutes of meditation daily.

The kale business had been steadily moving along, and we were doing six farmers markets a week that first season. I had done significant work on my credit that first year, thanks to my twelve step sponsor, and was able to get a loan for a used vehicle. The payments weren't ideal based on my credit score and history, but hey, most folx weren't willing to float me a cigarette a little over a year earlier.

During the remainder of October, my father had minimal time left, and my mother decided to bring him home for his final days. She had been disengaged from the pain pills since my last visit, and this plan with my Dad was likely the best for them both.

I spoke to him through the phone that last week even though he wasn't responding to my words. Through my practices I was preparing myself the best I could for the loss of a parent. I felt like I had barely found recovery in time to see him before dementia really wreaked havoc on his mind, so I was leaning into the practice and fellowships, sharing with others the challenges that I faced. It was almost harder to have him still here but not have him recognize anyone. It was hell, but I didn't have to do it alone.

On a Tuesday evening my mother called me while I was taking the bus back from the city.

"You should talk to your father for a few minutes, the visiting nurse doesn't think he'll make it through the night."

I don't remember much of what I said, other than I loved him and how I wished I could be there. Saying it all felt as though he was already gone.

When I woke up the next morning, the first information of the day prevalent through my phone updates was that Donald Trump had been elected president, and then I opened my email and there it was. An email from my mom to my siblings and I that my dad passed on sometime after midnight on Wednesday November 9th.

I had my regular scheduled service position and I stuck to it. Though I was deeply saddened by the loss of my father, there was no reason to deviate from my recovery routine. I remember finding it difficult to sit in my own skin in meditation; trying to be there with all of the sadness in my heart and anxiety in my belly of the upcoming trip home and all the communications and planning that it would require. Being a new business owner also meant I wouldn't get the opportunity to just take a couple days off to check out. I was going to have to get creative to walk through this and not take shortcuts. I had a meeting to secretary that night and I knew I needed to talk to those in the rooms who had experienced the loss of a parent.

Death always remains the greatest teacher because we are never prepared for the loss of a friend or loved one, no matter how much we can see it coming; everything shifts drastically within the relationships tied to that individual. We are forced to be with so much of the unsatisfactory nature of life when death occurs.

Again I leaned into the practice and my own resilience to guide me through this time. Mindful awareness of the emotions as they arose was key to understanding how to move forward. I probably learned more about myself and thought patterns during this time through practical application of labeling the emotional states and habitual thoughts as they showed up. When I found myself planning the trip home, unable to remain engaged in my forgiving myself for the hell I had been in the couple years before my father's passing, I called it what it was, "planning", then brought myself back to the phrases around my forgiveness practice. When I thought about no longer being able to talk to him, I named it "fear", felt the characteristics and sensations present, and again, came back to the breath as best I could.

Most importantly though, I saw this as an opportunity to ensure effective healing through mindful mourning, compassionate wishes for my family and their pain around this, and being in the discomfort of the impermanence of human life itself.

I thought about the feelings of my father's other children; my siblings that were now faced with no longer having a living parent, and what that pain must be like. Finding gratitude that I can still call my mother, and I can still help take care of her. Altogether, I was beyond thinking and feeling that I was the only one who experienced a loss here. I was able to see past my personal experiences and came to value the interconnectedness of friends and family during this time.

On Friday November 11th, Veteran's Day, the news special aired that had gathered footage from the last six months of my life, and it was bittersweet. I thought about how proud my father would have been if he could have seen it. I worked my ass off to get here, and this piece highlighted so much support from my community and the people around me. They had filmed a private yoga session I had with one of my favorite Seattle teachers, Kathleen Hunt. They came to the kale chip kitchen and discussed the process of going from addict to small business owner. It captured my drug court graduation, and lastly, some clips of my daughter and I walking on the beach.

I went home to Massachusetts for my father's services, and did not find it necessary to drink or use while I was there. It hadn't even crossed my mind. Plenty of my family members were drinking, and many others just went about medicating their grief, and I myself was fully content experiencing the waves of happiness and love, celebrating my father's life, as well as acknowledging the loss and disbelief that he was gone.

There was a beautiful service at the church that he attended as a child. Throughout all of it though I couldn't help but realize in my own healing from the end of my using, that I felt my concept of god was occasionally being led back to try and understand this Christian process, but I just couldn't wrap my head around the word "God".

The twelve step literature says, "God as we understood him", right there in the Third Step; and there's a whole section written on agnosticism. The truth of the matter is I wasn't understanding God, or a God, but I was experiencing something. Some process, or something had separated me from drugs and alcohol, and that's all I knew. But if addiction and alcoholism means a full flight from reality, then recovery for me had to be about being here now, connecting to this moment.

It didn't have to have anything to do with a higher power. There was surely surrender; surrender to this moment and the willingness to be with whatever is happening in it, without judgement. I am not just powerless over drugs and alcohol, I'm powerless over so much more. How I deal with that is by cultivating wise relationships and understanding with those areas in which I am powerless. Moving forward, having a friendly and kind, equanimous awareness with the present is how I translate the higher power piece and maintain my agency in the recovery process.

It's stated that lack of power is the problem, and the solution is a power; so at those moments when I'm able to be fully present, nonjudgmentally, I've tapped into the power necessary to maintain my recovery.

With that said, I have a deep appreciation for the twelve step programs and rooms. There was a continuum of experiences that led me to this mindful understanding in the personal program I work, and the rooms of AA/NA were an imperative component to the production of that.

In the beginning there was only Seattle PD, Major Crimes Task Force, the prosecuting attorney's office and its intervention that led to seeing Happy in the bullpen that day. Next came treatment, Buddhist teachings, literature and insights, and the yoga practices that I engaged in my cell, in tandem with the outpatient treatment, twelve step meetings and veterans program.

All of these contributed to my arriving at a place that I could figure out how to concoct a long term recovery program in the community, and appreciate all elements of my journey. Plus, I absolutely needed to work the steps, and I was willing to do so, even if I just believed the group itself was my conception of a higher power. Again, this is about connection, right? So I need to remain connected to the group of people doing this thing, staying sober, together.

I wasn't doing the "fake it 'til you make it", nope. I just understood that one size didn't fit all, and I had a breadth of support systems, and I was damn sure going to make them work. I had used quite the buffet of substances, and I was going to need a buffet of recovery if I was going to make this stick. Remember earlier when I mentioned the dope dreams in jail? I still get them from time to time, now over five years into my recovery. You know how many dreams I've had about getting clean in my life? Zero. That says a lot about how much the patterns and responses to a life of using have slipped into my subconscious, and about how much effort I ought to be putting into the work of mindfulness and my recovery.

But most of all, once I put all of this to work in my greater community, I am able to be in wise relations with myself through my sense of purpose in the world. This is the most important piece for me. After a while I began to understand who I am, how to tread the path forward, and who I want to be.

Truly understanding and valuing myself shows me I am so much more than who I was in my addiction, and I need those around me to understand that as well for me to thrive. I need the community, landlords and credit agencies to take a chance on me, and there's an urgency to stop measuring people by where they've been or who they were. At the beginning and end of the day we are all just human beings wrestling with aspects of ego, trying to get along in this world.

This brings me to the role of my stage characters. When I get up each day, there is a whole set of roles (or stage characters) that are part of a day in the life of Joe; and I may respond or react based on that character's own special set of circumstances.

For instance, it's a Monday. I get out of bed and the spiritual Joe gets up and practices yoga and a bit of meditation, and spiritual Joe is tied to the Joe in recovery, and that guy doesn't want to go back out and use (addict), so this is the daily reprieve of recovery contingent on spiritual connection. Next, there's the guy that showers, shaves and has breakfast while making his lunch, because he needs to make it through the workday, so here surfaces the employee. I kiss my spouse goodbye, because that's the guy in the relationship, and then I wish my daughter a good day at school, now that's the fatherhood role showing up.

I then jump in the car, or walk to the packed bus, doing my best to be kind while feeling short on personal space, and checking in on a mentee and watching the clock to see if I'm running on schedule; now enter the commuter, the mentor, and the employee again.

So right there, we already have a handful of different characters. Each one of them has its own fears and motivations. The guy that gets up and does the recovery practices doesn't necessarily share the identical fears as the fatherhood role in that moment, right? Surely I have concerns with keeping my sobriety, but are they the same concerns I have for my daughter as she heads off to school for the day, in a time when school shootings have become increasingly frequent across our nation? Not likely.

It is quite possible that some of these roles overlap while I'm immersed in any one of them. Yet, each of these roles has a separate set of relationships tied to it, and with them comes responsibility to those relationships. So if I get a call that my daughter is sick, and needs me to pick her up from school, there is a strong possibility I need to have a conversation with the boss (employee/employer), talk to my kid's mother (father/ex-partner) and tell my mentee that I'm not making the meeting tonight (recovery/mentor/mentee). Every one of those interactions could have me acting out on fears, ambition, and financial concerns because each character needs to show up differently. Yes, my addict ego is in there, always underlying, yet it's actually a just a sliver in reference to a holistic view of myself.

So at the end of the day, how much am I operating from the spiritual guy, the one connected to this moment, to himself, right now, the real Joe? I've got to make some time to nurture that relationship, because I've learned no one else is going to do it for me. I use the last 20-25 minutes of my lunchtime Monday through Friday, to do mindfulness/meditation practice. I do my best to remain present at that time to evaluate what stage characters have been at it today, and how they are showing up. Many times, I'm finding that I'm reactionary, but the goal here is to understand that's how I'm showing up. Once I know that it's happening, I'm presented with what I need to work with and be on the lookout for in the remainder of my day.

This way, with the proper connection to the best of my ability, no one needs to face the unchecked fears and unskillful aspects of my stage characters. I'm able to move forward, not back. I've come to experience that through a clear and accurate understanding of ego, I can live an extraordinary life on the inside. And if I can live like that internally, I will naturally live an extraordinary life externally as well.

15

Drug Court: From Participant to Peer

From the time I entered the drug court program, completed and had my felony charges dismissed, to the spring of 2017, I had endured significant challenges and successes. The next step was to figure out how to carry and share the tools and resources so that others may be afforded whatever liberation they could glean from my experiences.

Sometime during the winter of early 2017 I was approached by a local yoga instructor who saw the Veteran's Day piece when it aired. They work for a program that began in Washington State called Yoga Behind Bars.

YBB has been doing incredible work with incarcerated populations in the correctional facilities in our state for the last decade. They bring weekly classes to the county jails as well as state prisons, and offer trauma informed yoga instruction to those doing time.

There was a trauma informed weekend yoga training coming up in March, and based on my history having been previously incarcerated, there was a scholarship opportunity for me to attend the two and a half day training.

What an amazing gift! I was being offered training based on the fact that I had been behind bars for a period of time, not actually being denied access. I was starting to see beyond the conventional recovery concepts the multitude of ways in which I could help others.

At the training I was asked to share my experiences with the correctional system, and learned how I could apply my current teaching certification to bring yoga to marginalized populations.

My perspective on YBB's work was already wide open, having an understanding of what positive changes a yoga practice had done for my mental health when I was in jail.

The training was incredible, and there were a few other formerly incarcerated individuals that had found freedom through yoga and I was moved by the experiences of my peers. There were some in attendance too that were local instructors also understanding that our correctional system does not actually rehabilitate individuals, but only further perpetuates trauma and systems of oppression. They were there to learn the curriculum constructed by YBB staff so that they too could bring yoga instruction into the state's correctional entities and truly help those inside. They taught us about institutional racism and the impact on BIPOC folx in this time of mass incarceration with a breadth of resources and literature for self-reflection and education.

Following my drug court graduation, I had stayed in contact with the treatment program manager, Todd. I saw many current participants at the meetings around town, and I wanted to find a way to help them out. I heard pieces of my story in their shares, and I knew there had to be a way for me to be more effective than just trying to sponsor people once they made it into the rooms of recovery.

Throughout the meetings with Todd, we came to the conclusion that a drug court specific, peer run meeting may be of service to the participants, and we discussed different ways to implement that.

After a month of multiple ideas and frameworks, we had a sit down with the program manager and drug court judge at that time in early March. We all agreed it was a solid idea, and just needed to work through final details over the coming weeks.

Before I left the meeting that day Todd said, "Hey, FYI the resource specialist position is opening up, please let us know if you know anyone who'd be interested."

"Sure thing, is there a job posting for it?" I asked.

"Yeah, I'll forward it to you later today." Todd said.

The resource specialist role is a treatment agency contracted position that works out of the same office as the rest of the drug court team at the superior courthouse in downtown Seattle. The person in the position assists participants in everything from enrolling in Medicaid, obtaining clothing, getting ID, finding support meetings, employment and educational opportunities, and navigating and accessing other social services.

I started thinking about who I was familiar with and that would be a good fit for that role. After all when I got released, Dave, who was in that role, helped me get an ID and clothing within the first forty-eight hours I was out. The way the resource role interacts with clients is different from other staff roles, since they don't need to be monitoring treatment and urinalysis outcomes of the participant like case managers do. They really get to stay invested in specifically connecting the client to services and supports in the community that make navigating the rest of the program possible.

After looking at the job description for a few, it dawned on me that I actually had most of what they were looking for, except for the college degree part. But there was some language around lived experience.

When I got the chance to talk to Todd again, I brought up my interest in the position.

"I'd really like to apply for this spot, but I don't think I have all the desirables." I said.

"How so?" he asked. "You've utilized the services provided by that role and you're a successful graduate of the program. I think you have more than enough to offer, and even more so, you have a unique peer perspective with ability to understand where these clients are at. I'd encourage you to apply."

This was a difficult play. I had the kale business going strong with my family, but I just wasn't feeling complete in that work. Don't get me wrong, it was incredible from day one. But recently with the energy that had been sparked with Yoga Behind Bars and the news piece, I really wanted to get my foot in some work around behavioral health and helping others.

We had discussions around making it all fit, and since we were hiring employees to work markets I could tentatively come after finishing work at the court, and wrap up production at the kitchen afterward since it was only a ten minute bus ride from the courthouse.

After a week and a half and an interview, I was called and offered the position. The person who called to make the offer: my old outpatient substance use counselor; and though he was off-site at the treatment agency branch, he would be my supervisor.

I started the resource position with the drug court program in April of 2017, and since day one, it has not failed to fulfill my sense of purpose. I have managed to get up excited for that work day after day, for over three years now. My case manager Martin was no longer there when I started, but the rest of the team remained the same as when I was a participant. By the time I had spent slightly over one year in the position I went to a training and became a Washington State Certified Peer Counselor, and two months later picked up my Connecticut Community for Addiction Recovery (CCAR) Recovery Coach credential as well.

I understand that in the world of addiction and recovery, the criminal legal system plays a very controversial but important role; and in my case, that role saved my life. I started this book by stating that I was not writing anything to shift or direct your attention to the legal system as the solution, and I will remain true to my word, yet I'll explain how our drug court program works. It's also important that I acknowledge when I think of the program and how it works, I easily see myself as part of the team. Not because of the work I do, but because of how I identify. I'm still considerably young, a white male, and that privilege has afforded me to fit in on a treatment team made up primarily of white people, so even my participation in the program was easily culturally competent for my needs.

Looking at any programs that work with folx affected by SUD, MH challenges and trauma, they need to have direct representation of the communities and individuals they serve; one of the most important factors in establishing equitable treatment; and a thorough understanding of which communities of people have been historically most harshly impacted by harmful drug policy and racial disparities. This requires that therapists, counselors and other professionals hired to work in the field are actively working towards anti-racism and cultural humility, allowing for the clients themselves to be the experts in their lived experiences.

This program is one of the oldest drug courts in the nation, beginning in 1994. It is a felony diversion program, meaning that potential participants must be charged with an eligible felony for participation. The eligibility criteria has changed over the years, but has remained committed to serving the needs of the community based on the common criminalized activity surrounding or relating to substance use, or substance use fueled crimes. Common charges are vehicle prowl, vehicle theft and residential burglary, along with delivery (or selling/dealing) and some possession charges. It is not just about supporting recovery, but also behavior modification.

One motivator is that aside from receiving treatment, resources and maintaining abstinence, the client's felony or felonies are dismissed upon successful completion of the program. Since its inception, there have been over 2,500 graduates representing more than 2,700 dismissed felonies.

In the 1990's, Seattle saw a rise in crack cocaine related felonies from the War on Drugs. Drug Court began as a response to try and help people exit a life of substance dependence and drug dealing. It is an extremely collaborative team effort, including treatment staff and peers, prosecutors, defense attorneys and judges. For as much criticism of drug courts as I've heard around recovery communities, I've come to know that not enough folx have seen a treatment court in action that really adheres to evidence-based practices getting positive results for individuals, families and their surrounding community.

Our local program is generally a 12-18 month commitment. A full compliance participant can go through the five phases in twelve months or slightly less, while in many cases it will take about a year and a half, allowing time for treatment reengagement for a recurrence of use, relapse or set back due to missed groups/treatment obligations or new law violations.

Clients are required to attend an orientation and intake, get an overview of the program and its expectations, and meet with an appointed attorney. Most of this can happen in one day. Abstinence is not a requirement to attend the baseline obligations and get started in drug court, but it will be expected to further oneself along in the program, continuing on towards graduation.

Generally at the orientation, which occurs every Monday, I am the first one to introduce my role and what services I broker discussing everything from transportation provided by the program to setting appointments for doctor or dental referrals within the county's public health system.

I don't currently look much like the person I did in my active addiction, so I start my spiel with, "I am a graduate of this program, and I'm in long term recovery. I came into this program after sixteen years of active addiction for selling heroin to an undercover officer to support my habit. I'm here to offer services and experience, and if you would like to meet with me to discuss your program and resources needed, here's how you reach me."

At this time, the heads have usually lifted and I've caught some attention. I'd say two out of five times, there are faces in that room that I have met while I was out there in my addiction. The value in all of this is that they can feel like they have an ally in this process from the get-go. To me, the Monday orientations are like a fresh look at the research and development lab that lets me know things aren't getting any easier out there. Keep in mind, any folx that I recognize or vice versa have in many cases been out there living that life for the five plus years that I haven't; and just because I have the lived experience doesn't mean everything. Things have only gotten more difficult in the way of the addiction epidemic, and most of the people entering the program are polysubstance users of heroin/fentanyl, meth etc. The best I can do is to hope to level the playing field by talking the talk and when it comes down to it, sharing pieces of my story with them so they know I've really had to do this thing too. Nobody should have to figure out how to establish and work recovery alone. My terminal uniqueness had me walking the fine line between life and death those last couple years of my addiction, and I didn't know anything about peer support or recovery coaching until I was already a year plus into my recovery.

Once I'm done Shannon, the housing case manager, talks about his role and offers people to get on a waitlist for our single adult transitional housing program. The housing program, which is a recovery supportive model with some wiggle room for recurrence of use and reengagement, offers up to twelve months of stable, rent free housing in the community and is a collaboration with a couple of local organizations focused on helping folx with substance use, mental health challenges and reentry. There is also a family housing case manager that will work with parents or pregnant mothers to identify supportive housing or recovery programs in the community to support their needs. If we have clients living out of doors or in places not suitable for human habitation, housing case management can do a referral to a shelter bed close to the court program in the interim.

The rest of the morning is spent with a treatment case manager completing an assessment used to identify the level of care participants may benefit from while in the diversion program. When new clients leave our office they are given Narcan nasal spray, due to the understanding that many folx will have a difficult time becoming abstinent until starting medication or beginning treatment, so we focus on safer use and overdose prevention until the next steps can be taken as well as throughout a participant's time in the program.

Success is measured differently for many participants as the program offers multiple tracks. For instance there is a young adult model, designed to be effective with and addressing the needs and services for 18-25 year olds, also with its own single young adult housing. IOP is generally done in a setting with other young adults. There is a veteran's track, which can allow for treatment obligations and services to be met through the VA and has its own social worker available from the regional veteran's court program. And lastly, there is a COD, or co-occurring disorder track, tailored more toward the needs of client's with significant mental health in tandem with substance abuse, with its own housing models.

The assessment steers the level of care or appropriate treatment program for the individual, and most folx come away from the first day with an outpatient or mental health evaluation and intake scheduled at a provider in the community. Opiate dependent clients are offered the opportunity to get on medication to treat opiate use disorder if it appears to be a good fit, and a methadone, Suboxone or Vivitrol intake is scheduled. Many participants meet with me right after orientation and enroll in Medicaid, get a money order to replace their ID and are given hygiene supplies and bus tickets. All of this happens in the course of one morning.

Remember the TRP program? That too is one of the tracks for those that want to participate in drug diversion court but are at high risk/high needs and have difficulty stabilizing in the community.

This is where things tend to get crunchy in the debate about the most therapeutic process to effectively connect folx to treatment. Many say jail is not rehabilitating, and I agree. Was my continued staying in the community therapeutic? That wasn't leading me to treatment; and to be honest, it was killing me and I didn't have the courage to ask for help. Everyday behind bars at the TRP was far less traumatic than another day out in the streets, for me. I was already locked up in my own mind for the last sixteen years, and chances are, I'm not sure how many services I would have been connected to at any other agency in the community in the course of three and a half hours. Drug court's resources have been forged and nurtured over the last twenty-five years.

This is a heavy topic for many, the conversation of treatment in jail. Can people access substance use treatment in jail? Can they co-exist? The answer is yes, for now, and we are seeing it more on the national level as drug courts continue to receive bi-partisan support. Should all of these services be accessible for anyone in the course of a morning in every community across the country without jail? That answer is also yes. I don't believe people should serve time for drug use alone or simple possession; yet the hard facts are many of us commit crimes like vehicle prowl/vehicle theft, burglary and even robbery to support our use, and any program that only takes into consideration compassion for the addict and leaves out victims is not a truly well rounded program addressing *all* needs of the community. Homeowners and community members want answers and solutions; and I would be quick to think the person committing a burglary really doesn't want to do what they are doing. Like I said, nobody willingly signs up for living this way. It just becomes the cost of doing business to feel a little less pain. Behavioral health, social support, reentry services and reduced barriers still have to be part of their solutions, no matter the nature of the charges. Anyone can make a full U-turn in their path with proper support and resources; but most of all, one needs a life free from the limitations of conviction.

The level of risk and need deeming someone a potential fit for the TRP or an inpatient program has to be considered a substantial risk to themselves or the community, and have significant substance use or mental health needs, like was true in my case. With that said, drug court is not a fix all for every person with a substance use disorder, period; but it can and will work for many.

After clients engage in a few months of intensive outpatient treatment, random UA's, bi-weekly court hearings, and obtain some substantial distance from the lifestyle of using, they enter the Empowerment Plan part of our program that I discussed earlier. Many are still engaged in SUD/MH counseling one on ones, attending doctor's appointments etc. but the Empowerment Plan process begins to address outside areas needing support in the life of someone engaged in the program.

The layout of the Empowerment Plan has been updated since I came on board with the program. Shannon and I worked very closely to identify areas where we saw clients struggle and could benefit from understanding strengths, needs and next steps to specific areas in their life.

There are six categories: Recovery SUD/MH, Community/ Family Supports, Employment/Benefits, Housing, Education/ Training, and Health & Wellbeing. Most of these cover criminogenic risk/needs factors. After clients attend the class, they are expected to fill out the form in all six categories, to the best of their ability. After completion of that exercise, they schedule a sit-down and review of the categories with me.

Key thing here is there is no right or wrong way to do this; this becomes a living document for their remaining time in the program. The judge and the rest of the team will use this material to help support and encourage the individual in accessing and following through on ways to stay engaged in their recovery and remain disengaged from self-identified harmful behaviors. Lastly, we are able to find out where people still need support. For instance, we might discover in the process that an individual has an eviction on their housing record, and we now have an opportunity to provide support and resources to help address that before they get too far from the program. The goal is always to help folx depart from the program in better circumstances than the way they came to us.

Everyone has their own specific story and needs to address as it relates to their personal journey. I see all kinds of different backgrounds in education, employment and housing, and in general at this point in the program, the recovery process presents itself fairly similarly for most participants. In many of the focus areas, clients are now able to understand the strengths, needs/risks and next steps to build a stable foundation on.

The one area that tends to be stressed the most, and a handful of clients have a difficult time completing, is the Community/Family Support category. Unless the person is particularly young, this one area often appears, at first, as irreparable. Many are alienated from their families and friends, do not have natural support systems, burned bridges with employers and landlords, and outside of the court program's fellow participants and newly discovered recovery community, they are detrimentally lacking.

Why is that?

My opinion is that this is a byproduct of the societal view and response to addiction and the stigma around it. Many times it's because of their involvement in the criminal legal system that their community would choose to distance themselves from people like us. I was denied a housing opportunity while in the program due to the fact that I had pending felony charges. Things sorted themselves out eventually, but again I was also a thirty-two year old white male. I didn't exactly fit the bill of the widely stigmatized addict once I got into recovery; my physical appearance had improved and the felony was dismissed. The path out was far less challenging for me; and because disparities exist we need to address and dismantle stigma and systemic racism, all the while understanding how they have affected treatment access, medical services and general community recovery and wellbeing.

All of this work is crucial to the success of our communities as a whole. Without healthy relationships with ourselves and neighbors, we are all destined to pursue relationships with inanimate objects like substances or behaviors, which inevitably lead us further away from one another and into a cycle of addiction.

In my work as a peer counselor with drug court clients, I have conversations with folx when they first begin or again after a recurrence of use or relapse. My first question is usually, "Who were you with or who do you spend your time with?" or "How were you feeling when this happened?" Nine times out of ten, the answer is they were emotionally fucked up or isolated; involving situations and people with similar coping mechanisms and habit patterns; so how would they not use?

So the question arises, if we are able to get folx on any path separated from drugs and alcohol for a period of time, and then there is a recurrence of use, what element of treatment is missing?

The answer is in work that does not put all of the onus on the individual, but rather on the community. If we have a society that dislocates people faster than it can treat, house or assist them, people are far more likely to develop unskillful relationships with substances or behaviors. The response needs to be in addressing the systems that continuously oppress and dislocate people like capitalism, racism, classism, sexism.

How many future addicted populations are being born out of our policies of separating children from their parents at the border? How many people will find relief in substances when they are displaced by gentrification, rising rent costs and lower wages in places like Seattle, San Francisco, LA and other major cities?

We wholesale manufacture addiction in the United States from Big Pharma to our high speed lifestyles, destructive late stage capitalism and its offshoots like mass incarceration. We ourselves are addicted to creating generations of suffering populations and then blaming them for being human and seeking relief from a painful existence.

The work to be done is ours to own and act on. In the process of expecting others to "act right" we need to learn to do the same, and in Seattle alone there are many agencies and groups to listen to already taking the lead on transforming our community approaches and responses.

One of the benefits of witnessing participants progress in our program is watching them build up their recovery capital. For many, this begins with educational and employment opportunities in agencies focused first on mitigating the challenges of living with SUD, being system involved or system impacted. Some second chance employers have created a workplace culture of self-empowerment through collaborative team efforts and hiring events. In our area alone there a handful of city agencies, area colleges and regional employers that are getting people connected to education and back to work as direct reflections of needs seen in our immediate communities.

Recovery high schools, collegiate recovery programs, and recovery drop in centers have gained incredible momentum letting us know that our communities see us, understand social and generational impacts, and are here to support us. Legislative forums, SUD/MH advocacy days at the state capitol and local recovery conferences are putting our faces at the forefront of change. Washington Recovery Alliance and regional recovery coalitions are making strides in our local arena around public policy, understanding and engagement.

It's up to us and the larger community members to become aware of what is working and how in other regions and put that to work in our own neighborhoods. I'm seeing more recovery advocacy and Naloxone trainings in my home county in Western Massachusetts, with groups finding ways to get funding and start programs while understanding how overdose reversal medications work in the interim. A two-fold process of saving lives in any community invested in long-term solutions.

Yes things are missing and more can always be done, but I'd also like to point out that we are headed in a direction that is normalizing addiction to a place where people can fit in and be accepted.

I think much of this can be attributed to the increasing support of Peer Counseling/Recovery Coaching in treatment and recovery planning. As mentioned from my own experience in assisting clients in our program, when someone can walk the path alongside the newcomer to recovery, their opportunities at sustaining that recovery increase.

I'm able to say to clients, "Hey, I'm hitting this meeting or meditation tonight, and there'll be some people there. You could come and check it out if you'd like. I'll be there at seven." they get an opportunity to be part of something again, something new, and something communal that has long term positive effects on their lifestyle and ability to re-establish their place in the world, and they feel thought of. Sure, I had plenty of suggestions from the court, but the rubber really met the road when others in recovery showed me how to do this thing rather than told me how. I also acknowledge that my being a peer in a court program may not be seen as effective as a peer relationship built specifically outside of the legal system, yet it is a far more effective approach than one with an absence of lived experience.

The power of the peer perspective will become the strongest tool in the years to come in overhauling how we treat and interact with addiction. The beauty of this is that it will always embrace the idea that no one size fits all, because it will employ different walks of recovery rather than just one program or modality. Doing away with the idea that if someone can't conform or "make it" in x, y, or z program, they are service or treatment resistant. That mindset and harmful, stigmatizing language is what's keeping people out there dying and not getting the treatment they need.

Doing peer work is slowly dismantling the pieces of misunderstanding anonymity that have hindered true progress and healing in our communities. It sheds light on the different programs and paths towards whatever freedom looks like for an individual, so long as we remain open minded of what recovery can be, and not what one believes it isn't.

This is where outcomes come into play. I mentioned that drug court isn't for everybody, just like some recovery programs aren't for everybody either.

I personally believe recovery to be "any process or program, completely abstinent or not, that nurtures agency in one's life back over to them to make informed decisions to improve their quality of life without furthering self-destruction from substances or behaviors". Of course this description doesn't fit precisely into diversion courts, but we're also not the only path to recovery in town; and sustained abstinence isn't the only benefit of completing the program.

For some of our folx, just getting the felony charge(s) dismissed is the goal of participation in the drug court program, but it still requires a similar level of commitment. Often it's the lifestyle that gets people here; the fast money of dope dealing and trafficking stolen property, so occasionally landing someone in a long term vocational or trade program that can give them a consistent income and fulfilling role is their motivation to change. I don't need to impose how I think one could benefit by having a goal of abstinence or recovery; I can still be effective in sharing my experience in the process of attaining goals and navigating setbacks associated with personal growth and success.

As for drug court and leading up to participant graduation, the most fruitful outcomes I see are with clients that have been able to consistently identify and cultivate supportive community. Whether it's through amending relationships, becoming a good employee, getting their children back, or becoming the primary caretaker of a parent, the main ingredient here is that they find purpose through their personal lens and that of the community.

Once in a while clients do return on an arrest, sometimes even within a year, but the common denominator is generally the absence of purpose and community. "I was hanging out with my old friends" or "I graduated from the program and didn't pursue employment." Whatever the case may be, something related to positive community and support is usually missing. Ongoing success and progress are dependent on the building and maintenance of supportive communities.

Over the last three and a half years, I've had five or six drug court graduations where I've had the honor of introducing someone that I had been out there with. Going from standing on the corner of Second and Pike smoking crack at two in the morning, to side by side in recovery at graduation is probably the best high I've ever had.

16

Epilogue-A Path Forward

Five years after my last arrest, I rarely think about drugs and alcohol. I occasionally have dreams of use, but I take that as expected after fifteen plus years of ingesting intoxicants during most of my waking moments.

Rachael and I separated a couple of years back, and she continues to run the kale business. My partner April and I were married in August of 2020, and we split care and time with my daughter, all living in Seattle.

I'm at a point where I don't frequent the twelve step rooms anymore, and have been steadily working a Buddhist recovery program for the last three years; because just like my addiction progressed, so has my recovery. I've found that the process I worked and things I did in the first years of my sobriety are not what's needed to maintain my recovery as it is today.

I'm now at a place where I am striving to understand this world and my relationship to it. It's no longer about my relationship with substances; it hasn't been for some time. Not that any program is better or less effective than another, but because I have personally found it necessary to work with a different lens at times, because it's important to be able to shift perspective for renewed effectiveness. In attaining my goals, I've deepened my mindfulness and meditation practices, sat a handful of silent Vipassana retreats ranging from three to ten days, mentoring folx in early recovery, and I continue to share my experience at the regional level. Without negotiation I practice yoga and meditation almost daily, facilitate recovery support groups for clients, teach mindfulness and write about my life experiences.

As for the world around me, there are difficult conversations about treatment and addiction to have in our community that require we broaden our view; to get outside of rigid beliefs limiting our ability to treat one another compassionately.

I'm often asked what I think would be effective or helpful in the efforts to reduce the impact of addiction in our communities. For starters, my personal praise of the police interventions that saved my life are nowhere near as pronounced as they were when I was getting my shit together; simply because that approach is just not helping enough people, and in many cases actually causes more harm.

I also wonder as to why some folx in the larger recovery community are at war with each other over which program people should be working, feeling compelled to argue why one path is better than another? Abstinence is just not always going to be the goal, and harm reduction will not always be appropriate, end of story. My journey may be similar to yours, but explicitly it is not yours, and vice versa. Haven't we spent enough time at war with ourselves in our addiction that we should just focus on how our lived experiences can serve the next suffering individual; sharing that we should expect recovery, that it is possible even if it isn't our brand; and that the quality of one's life can improve over where it currently is?

To be clear, I'm not locked in or fully convinced that the following ideas are *the* way. Everything is subject to change; we need to be prepared to reevaluate and refine policies and methods, and based on my personal values and experiences, these are the practices and concepts that I believe will help us tread a positive path forward.

Let's look at decriminalization.

Decriminalization can positively serve the population affected by substance use disorder, as well as the taxpayer, *but not in every instance.* For all intents and purposes, we spend less time and money on the process of arrest, booking and housing in correctional facilities while also keeping us in line with medicalizing addiction as a disease; rendering treatment as a solution by no longer viewing the individual affected as a criminal, but rather as a person or patient needing care.

The catch is that adulterated narcotics used can include more lethal substances like fentanyl and are not regulated. The urgent task with any decriminalization approach along with producing a safer supply is that we have to atone for the mass incarceration of communities of color from the overall war on drugs, and the others affected by draconian drug policy historically driven by fear, stigma and misinformation. More importantly, the legalization of drugs like heroin, cocaine, MDMA, and marijuana is a necessary step, while creating safer access to the drugs that people use because they are going to use them, whether we get behind that reality or not. Whether it be prescribed heroin and/or the guided therapeutic use of plant-based healings like Ayahuasca, safe supply and access to continuing care is a necessity. Bear in mind that overall decriminalization is the right step, but let's be clear: there is nothing radical or innovative about it when an approach leaves people in bondage to substances without increasing accessibility to resources and funding treatment appropriately to undo the underlying causes and conditions.

In addition, multiple housing resources in the local landscape have shifted to a "housing first" model, which says you don't need to be clean and sober, or in most cases what is considered to be abstinent. This results in ongoing substance use in some housing programs, but at least gets folx in doors, and there's an opportunity to then connect them to resources or care. In light of this, for those that want to work a completely substance free program certain housing options will be off the table.

Let's look at medication briefly, or commonly referred to as MAR (Medication Assisted Recovery) or MAT (Medication Assisted Treatment). Medications for addiction treatment are an evidence based approach, most commonly used in treating opiate use disorder, which is often prescribed through medications like Methadone, Buprenorphine (Suboxone) or Vivitrol. Some require daily doses and others may be less frequently administered; as little as once a month in the case of Vivitrol. For anyone unfamiliar, MAR is a tool and pathway that can transition individuals in active opioid use to a medication that can help prevent overdose and begin to facilitate their recovery process. It also supports moving the individual away from the currently criminalized behaviors associated with procuring substances.

Some abstinence advocates and abstinence-based recovery programs discourage the use of medications, while others encourage its use with an eventual transition off, but there's overall reception in the greater recovery community. My personal view is if someone's quality of mind and body are improving, recovery is happening; again regardless if one is totally abstinent and/or utilizing medication.

I consider myself in abstinence-based recovery, continuing to find it unnecessary to take the full flight from reality through drugs or alcohol. Many twelve step programs and mutual support groups have set this precedent decades ago, claiming complete abstinence or renouncing mind-altering chemicals as the way out. Often these programs declare that for things to actually change, for one to lose the desire to use, they must have a kind of psychic change or spiritual awakening, often found by working steps or committing to some kind of process, while not consuming substances. It's important to add that many people have "recovered" or renounced drugs/alcohol after a life-changing event, existential wake-up call or interaction with law enforcement, not once stepping foot in a mutual support or twelve step group, and never touching substances again. The truth is that a handful of people simply grow out of their unskillful relationship to substances and many folx can work towards and achieve abstinence, so long as they identify purpose and receive encouraging community and family support.

I do believe abstinence should be the focus for our teen and young adult populations if we have the ability to introduce positive peer influence to the individual in settings like young people's meetings, youth drop-in centers and recovery high schools. As for those individuals who have spent decades using and are heavily dislocated socially, economically and also in matters of health, harm reduction practices would likely be the more compassionate and realistic approach while working closely with them to find some form of social stability.

For years the treatment and direct services landscape has been saturated with pockets of individuals either in or heavily focused on abstinence-based recovery, employed as treatment providers or counselors in the field of addiction. In recent years, some of the more orthodox counselors appear to be thinning as the lean towards increased harm reduction practices has led to the abstinence-driven professional's services becoming less relevant as conventional forms of addiction treatment evolve to serve and also address the needs of individuals who cannot stop using, and are still deserving of care. We are seeing more peer based services, as well as a wave of younger, more open-minded addiction professionals capable of working with and supporting an individual, whether or not abstinence is the goal.

As decriminalization picks up speed, one other item I've encountered is that it can be increasingly challenging for some early along abstinence-based individuals to watch drug use happening openly in public, when in a treatment setting it is often encouraged that clients become aware of their triggers, abstain from use, and stay away from old hangouts. The fact is that both abstinence and reducing harm will continue to coexist, and they each require different treatment modalities and clear, concise messaging to the public to be supportive of the individual working each respective process. It will be a balancing act for communities to establish multi-pronged approaches effectively and empower individuals on whichever course they choose; offering path supportive housing, ongoing treatment and safer use supports along the way like supervised consumption spaces and unadulterated substances, all to increase public health.

What about policing and involvement in the criminal legal system?

As a city, Seattle has claimed to be moving to stop trying to arrest its way out of addiction, and nationally other cities are trying to decriminalize or move away from the war on drugs as well. Are arrests of addicted populations still occurring? Yes. Let's dig a little deeper into how this currently looks in my area.

In 2020 on a scale of public safety, it may be safe to say that low level drug dealing, sex work, possession and personal use of narcotics equates to a small nuisance; minor intervention required. Negligible harm done, outside of to the individual. Though it's a difficult sight for some, these are not heinous acts. Enter LEAD (Law Enforcement Assisted Diversion or soon to be reworked as Let Everyone Advance with Dignity, in Seattle) programs for these instances and a low expectation of abstinence. In short, local needle exchange programs, HIV/Hep C testing, overdose prevention, fentanyl testing strips and services focused on survival sex workers go hand in hand with this decriminalization/harm reduction approach to reduce risks to the individual and improve public health.

Programs like our local drug diversion court are designed and reworked as necessary to be responsive to the needs of the community, and continue to evolve as those needs shift. When it began in the mid 90's, it was intended to connect individuals living with addiction to treatment and seen as a means to divert folx away from incarceration. Twenty-five years later it still serves the same purpose, and though it aims to work with higher risk and higher needs individuals it doesn't totally keep addicted people out of going to jail or prison.

Today, a substantial amount of charges entering our drug court are crimes fueled by substance use disorder, like possession of stolen motor vehicles, vehicle prowl, residential burglary and some selling/dealing charges. So for the most part, the program takes in property crimes. Scale of public safety consideration? Remember, now we have other community members affected. The intervention required in this scenario equates to intermediate/elevated. This model separates the individual from substances, possibility of minimal jail time and restitution to the victim(s). There is an expectation of compliance or adherence to a behavior modification program; also to reintegrate and build positive community. Felony charges are dismissed upon completion of the program, usually 12–18 months after arraignment. Along the way behavioral health treatment, housing and a multitude of other resources are offered.

The main area of concern in treatment courts that requires evolution is the sad truth that too often these programs operate from a place that attempts to treat substance use disorder as a disease until one day it doesn't. At some point, the individual doesn't or can't meet the expectations of the program, and we resort back to the punitive measure of sentencing, and the participants then live with conviction. This has to change; we cannot bounce between the disease model and moral failing mentality and consider this practice progressive.

There is also a local family treatment court program that identifies the risk of substance using parents in the role of the family unit. In general, the state and CPS are already involved, so this becomes another case of intermediate/elevated risk, and program adherence and abstinence are required. Program graduation/case dismissal entails a child returning to home with the parent in recovery.

Lastly, in the criminal legal system as it addresses addiction, we have substance use related assaults, robberies and a handful of other personal crimes. Intervention required could be considered severe. These charges generally go to a regular mainstream court, rather than a diversion program, at least locally. This begins with the removal of the individual from the community, and incarceration and/or long term behavior modification programs may be implemented. Abstinence is generally expected and there may be attempts to address substance use, mental health and other underlying contributing factors, with an intent to eventually reintegrate the individual to the community. The truth is those programs associated with mainstream courts heavily isolate people from any supportive community and often don't produce effective change or rehabilitation. Finally, healthy reintegration, or reentry as it's often referred to, rarely occurs due to one having to live with conviction and its associated stigmas.

Compassion with the appropriate application of accountability can often produce great outcomes, yet accountability doesn't have to only exist in the legal system for it to work positively. Accountability needs to be cultivated in our community and healthcare systems to maintain a positive intention to help those struggling around us by no longer throwing them away into the systems as we do. This will require us to take up accountability to each other to create change, rather than pawning it off on broken systems expecting people to change in them. The old definition of insanity; doing the same thing over and over, expecting different outcomes. We could move towards legalization, generating a safer supply of narcotics, and in doing so could alleviate the pressures that motivate one to commit property crimes to come up with the means to procure substances and meet their basic needs. It's just seemingly ridiculous to continue down the same path we have, potentially prosecuting simple possession, retail theft and other considerably innocuous behaviors associated with obtaining drugs when there are alternative approaches.

The reality is this: everyone requires a different type of intervention or approach, and right now, Seattle and some other cities are operating from a place that says we are going to meet people where they are at in an irrational, half-assed decriminalization approach, which has unintended consequences. Yes, we say we're meeting them where they're at; but the truth is it is continuing to keep some people where they're at. In my case my family, friends, and recovery community all wanted more for me, because they knew I was capable of more than barely surviving and using; and the truth is that everyone is capable of more. What we are doing is allowing ourselves to openly oppress the population challenged with their behavioral health, by not encouraging *any* kind of path forward, mostly because we don't have them available for the population with multiple and/or severe needs. To be honest, our current decriminalization approach has shortchanged some folx of an intervention that could have otherwise helped them into a process of recovery and improved their circumstances, by leaving them in the streets under the guise of the desire to participate in programs or treatment solely up to and resting on them. We know that racial disparities, trauma and criminal histories create barriers in access to proper treatment and social services, and those needing a higher level of care and extended support just don't get it and are literally left in the cold. Though many affected individuals get acknowledged of needing treatment, it's all too often not just and equitable, or appropriate. The truth is we simply do not fund treatment and recovery programs similar to the way we don't fund education and other community based programs; too much money goes into policing to corral and manage those living with SUD and mental health challenges, and the marginalized and vulnerable often remain that way.

Disinvesting in militarized policing and moving that money into education, cultural and ethnic community building, anti-racist, anti-discriminatory education and practices and community based health and healing services, like increased access to treatment and paying for schooling and licensure/certification of people to help is a good start.

We can begin by bringing intermediate drug related crimes before a panel including legal representation, peers, and behavioral health specialists, like a substance use disorder professional and licensed mental health counselor, and get baseline assessments while establishing ongoing, long term support. We need to know what the individual's causes, conditions and immediate needs are, separate from a blanket approach. Our county jail systems need to be transformed to actually offer solutions to the high percentage of people currently behind bars or in the system that live with mental health issues and/or substance use disorder, while working to completely do away with less harmful drug related incarceration and past convictions.

So for starters, we need to not put people into jail or prison for their use, but rather convert or entirely rebuild existing county jail facilities into proper treatment and public health agencies focused on current and recovering drug user health. Doing away with the carceral system, we build them out with an intermediate risk treatment program and collaborative resources such as parenting classes, local employment and housing workshops; tangible tools for healing like one on one therapy, peer counseling, and mindfulness meditation programs. Many of our population affected by SUD/MH are living out of doors, are parents and family members, and we owe them the possibility of being in the life of their loved ones. Housing is a human right, and so is family reunification, a livable wage job or disability income that is in line with the cost of living in that city or county. Meanwhile, we rework the larger state facilities into longer-term programs for the more severe victim-related drug offenses, still doing away with the carceral, traumatic environments associated with conventional in custody facilities. Onboard peers with lived experiences in exiting the current criminal legal system as we know it, furthering personal development to help those new to the programs, all with the same intermediate level offerings; doing away with stacks of years behind bars as an attempt to forget about people until their release dates without providing the necessary tools for healing. Also, completely eradicating youth detention, and working towards positive peer, family and community support through the power of story and transformation by those that have come before them. Get people connected and get them the treatment and support they need that restores agency to them as an individual. We have whole communities and their families to be responsible for, not just a population of affected individuals. We need holistic approaches, taking into consideration the impact addiction and mental health have on the family unit and society and generations before and generations to come. Punishing people for substance use through incarceration is hopeless; as addiction punishes those living with it through every moment of every day.

Of course there is a sliver of the population that will commit violent crimes, requiring incarceration, supervision, and removal from the community, but that number dwarfs the number of folx behind bars for drugs and drug related offenses.

Money going to programs must be respective of the number of clients and the level of care and needs served. It's just being realistic that we don't go all in on funding one approach to address a large societal, human condition affecting diverse populations. Again, divesting in policing has to happen; spending more year over year on law enforcement has never lowered the drug supply and use, and incarcerating people adversely affects public health outcomes and only perpetuates addiction and mortality rates. When adjusted, local budgets must move money directly from policing to invest in the diversity of the community, rather than dumping funds into racist, classist policing, the drug war, and the role of police or school resource officers in the school to prison pipeline.

Specific circumstances require distinct solutions. Speaking to the people experiencing homelessness in King County alone, this means 12,000 plus individual sets of circumstances that require attention in our community, many of those involve substance use disorder and mental health.

We need to ensure professionals in the field like counselors and peers are paid livable wages so they can continue to commit their lived experience and/or professional energy, efforts and services to this work that many other people are simply not capable of providing. Again, funding redirected from policing should be put into community focused programs with targeted outcomes for those historically affected the most by the drug war and police brutality, like BIPOC folx and low income neighborhoods, ensuring that BIPOC led organizations are able to secure funds for treatment and programs directly serving them and that their voices are always represented and elevated, especially when making or overhauling policy.

Furthermore, this approach will also require that we dismantle the harmful role of the child welfare system and social workers. Current conversations around divesting from policing have abruptly jumped to passing the torch of numerous interventions over to social workers without fully acknowledging the existing harmful aspects of whiteness in social work. This reaches into addressing and unpacking the damages caused by child protective services (CPS), its agents and racist impact; another aspect of the carceral regime setting up many communities for family separation, intergenerational trauma and addiction.

We must continue to operate from the understanding that far too many contemporary police are not agents of treatment and recovery to those that need it most. They are simply not trained to address SUD and mental health crises while carrying firearms, frequently identifying people as threats rather than someone in need of help.

Lastly, it's imperative to acknowledge the need to remove a substantial scope of treatment for SUD/MH from the criminal legal system, finally placing it in the hands of communities and local healthcare systems with treatment and community court collaboration, as necessary. Any reliance on the criminal legal system should be utilized as an intervention with increased accountability for the intermediate/elevated risk, victim involved crimes associated with SUD like residential burglary and vehicle prowl/theft etc.

Remember, nothing changes if nothing changes.

Other items worth keeping in mind

Considering all we know about the progressive nature of substance use disorder and the studies about ACEs (adverse childhood experiences) and trauma, we need to remember that living out of doors and/or being in active addiction subjects one to a continued cycle of trauma.

When it comes to the housing crisis, it's not an easy adjustment to begin living inside once a person has been out of doors for extended periods of time. Keys to a new place won't solve everything, and in some cases, it makes matters more challenging for individuals. Many people experiencing homelessness use stimulants to remain in a state of hypervigilance during potentially unsafe times, like late at night and early morning hours. Once one gets indoors we need to work with them towards achieving a sense of safety and security during those difficult hours. Furthermore, in the community, housing with a behavioral health treatment component has to be accessible. So naturally we should be looking to empower individuals by not just meeting people where they are at, but asking them where they want to be throughout the process of engagement.

At large in our society, we have a tendency to identify and reference people in three ways; and commonly resort to measuring them using only numbers one and two.

1. What we "think to be true"; often based on previous, potentially outdated information. This can be rooted in stigma and harmful labeling.
2. What's true of them currently; accurate person-centered representation of their present situation.
3. Where that person would like to be; a vision based on empowerment and restoring agency to the individual.

To adopt more of numbers two and three, we must drop labels like "felon", and "addict" etc. and believe in the use of positive language to engage and empower others and ourselves, in an effort to envision a future rather than measure one's past. Using person-first language like "person seeking treatment" "person living with an SUD", "person seeking employment", and so forth.

With that said, it's going to be a challenge to look with hope to any model operating in an economic system that can't support its citizens' human rights. Basic needs (food, water, shelter) must be met for an effective large scale decriminalization and harm reduction approach to truly work. It's also just the right thing to do. Addiction and mental health are going to continue as long as humans walk the earth, and as long as systems like privatization and capitalism continue to displace those in lower socioeconomic status, unnecessary pain will be sought to be medicated. We should be creating safe consumption spaces for people to engage in the behaviors they will, and that absolutely has to begin with those basic needs being met. In the city, in those housing programs that do permit substance use and offer client services, it can be manageable. But we have 12,000 plus unhoused residents in our county, and I can tell you from personal experience it's very difficult not to use drugs for relief when you don't have a roof over your head. It is my role as the individual to understand and respect the needs and concerns of my community, as some didn't feel safe in my presence while I was in my active use. I am responsible for undoing that, and to do so, the community is responsible for providing the means necessary for this to occur. Constant re-evaluation of the needs of the individual and community are required moving forward; therefore adopting an approach resembling the Portugal Model has gone long overdue. It's time to heal the intolerance, misinformation and stigma about addiction in our communities.

To do this and turn the tide, those of us compelled and willing to fight for change like we have fought for our own lives or those of our loved ones, need to bring our efforts to change the system that keeps us in constant crisis. There are complex, oppressive systems that operate and are supported by both sides of the political aisle as it sits. A true path forward comes from realizing that our contemporary political system, with its ideologies and so called values, has always contributed to the detrimental conditions and disparities of racism, classism, and sexism that lead members of every community and identity to find comfort in substances and behaviors. Addiction affects every individual regardless of race, culture, belief or identity. So no, it is not enough to just vote our way out of problems and into long term solutions through Republican or Democratic parties as they exist. Historically, both parties and its supporters have been responsible for the decimation of BIPOC communities, as well as further marginalization of populations that have been stigmatized through addiction and class status.

Now in recent years with the flooding of prescription opioids, the white community has finally been affected enough to get bipartisan support for less harmful policy and approaches to treatment, community support and understanding. That has only further shed light on the preexisting disparities, stigmas, and fear that ravaged BIPOC communities. But the problem is, when it comes to politics, most Americans operate much like the drug addict, accepting whatever relief they can as elections near, settling for little to no change in policy. To begin unpacking it, this work must start at the local level by getting the faces of addiction and recovery into policy meetings, town halls and eventually into the regional political landscape as elected officials. We cannot allow decisions to be made absent of our voice at those tables and discussions. As it's said, nothing about us, without us. We cannot let up in the recovery advocacy movement; we must understand that we are fighting for our lives and the lives of others when it comes to substance use disorder. This is where it's imperative to address SUD as a condition to be treated rather than a moral failing; and we have research pointing to it as a brain disease. This is one gateway in which we get closer to treatment on demand. It has to be viewed as such to get people needing and wanting treatment the most into a place in which they can receive the appropriate care, choosing to participate in a path(s) that is the best fit with support from holistic teams outfitted with recovery coaches/peer support counselors to help regain control of our lives and our minds and bodies. Again, the true experts and professionals in this setting are those with the lived experiences that have made it out of the trenches, with the ability to show people how to recover rather than tell them how.

So as I write the closing of this book, serving as a peer counselor and social services specialist, the world is in the midst of the COVID-19 pandemic and protests of the murders of Ahmaud Arbery, Breonna Taylor, and George Floyd and many others by white men and law enforcement.

COVID-19 is a disease that is festering in the US due to the same political and economic systems that have continued to fail people that live with the dis-eases, struggle and stigma associated with addiction, mental illness, the criminalization of poverty and homelessness, and last but surely not least to be mentioned, the dis-ease of being non-white in this country. COVID-19 appears to be winning a war on America the same way opioids waged war and secured ongoing victory over rural communities in the nation for the last two and a half decades. The healthcare systems that should be in place and designed to serve and treat people affected by the coronavirus are practically non-existent, and this sprouts from the system failing those most susceptible to succumb and die because of the lack of an emergency response, mirroring the handling of substance use disorder for decades. Whole communities are now at the mercy of a system that doesn't see or value them, running contrary to what some of us, especially white folx, thought all along.

Imagine if we had slowed court proceedings, let nonviolent offenders out of jail and mobilized resources in response to the addiction crisis the way we mobilized and halted aspects of life as we know it for the coronavirus. Our nation's leaders knew the destructive potential of the virus that was unfolding, and in many cases were unwilling to respond effectively; leaving many Americans jobless, penniless and hopeful for government assistance to ease the blow of the impact on our immediate communities. All of this is much of the same to how states, cities and residents still await settlements and resources to fund treatment and offset the havoc wreaked by the opioid epidemic.

We also weren't prepared to properly support the new and existing recovering communities because the inequity cracks became even more pronounced in light of COVID-19. Due to social distancing, recovery support meetings and treatment groups have gone online, requiring people to have access to computers or smartphones. Against popular belief, these are luxury items accessed by or belonging to people of privilege, and are not easily attainable by the still suffering addict, person completing inpatient treatment or already vulnerable/marginalized populations. Because we have never had a proper response to the addiction crisis, many in our communities never anticipated the compounding health risks some would endure during COVID-19; expecting patients receiving medication (such as methadone, Suboxone, medication management programs for individuals with mental health challenges) to have to continue to go back into urban, often densely populated areas to obtain vital medications. All of this is unacceptable, and it happens solely because profit has more value than human life in this nation's capitalist system.

At the onset of COVID-19, our communities engaged in conflict at Costco and local markets over toilet paper and hand sanitizer, grasping to whatever felt sense of relief can come from hoarding just enough steaks and TP to not feel the pain of the world collapsing around us. The large scale dis-ease, unrest and fear associated with the unknown has brought out the worst of craving in all of us. As coronavirus has progressed, in some circles and in the spirit of selfishness with a complete disregard for science, it has brought out an inflated apathy for others in our communities, very similar to the attributes of substance dependent individuals. The American way of life as we know it, now in its rawest form, has finally exposed the heartbeat of addiction that is alive and well in our society.

Though there has been widespread acknowledgement that addiction is extremely common in the US, thanks to the pharmaceutical industry and drug cartels that have preyed on life lived "the American way" (treating symptoms instead of causes and conditions; and an instant gratification to feel anything but the way I'm feeling right now) we have come to know that there is no money to be made for the ruling class in healthy, safe and secure people. Many of us not already strung out on substances or behaviors are addicted to the slow death of fast, hard American living. Therefore, to actually further prevent friends and family from experiencing addiction, we will require much more of a radicalized movement that upends the current system ensnaring us in cycles of repetitive craving, like hamsters on the endless wheel. This is not something that can be done by supporting the same politicians representing the same two party bullshit. That system will not agree to a drug model like Portugal's when it fuels itself off of the profits of human misery and suffering in systems meant to serve corporate interests; not us. True prevention can only come from undoing the unjust systems and conditions we are forced to live and operate under in a capitalist nation.

I see people representing the recovery movement that call themselves advocates, asking others to openly support whatever politician on the bigger tickets is willing to acknowledge that addiction is a crisis. I'd like to say "yes, I support that", but it's just not good enough; shit, we've barely been able to get cities and counties to acknowledge racism as a public health crisis in response to increased video recorded violence against BIPOC folx. Sure these actions take some hold locally, but beyond the state level, how far have we gotten? What has really changed for the better in response to 67,000 plus deaths from overdose in 2018 alone?

How about supporting the politicians most vocal about undoing the systems that keeps us looking for refuge in drugs and alcohol? Actually working to elevate the people and voices that have experienced this broken system and understand it cannot be reformed from within, and therefore has to become a different system. Why continue to settle for politicians that have perpetuated addiction? Both parties regularly force feed us candidates that have been responsible for maintaining white supremacy, the war on drugs and destroying generations and communities to line their pockets and maintain office.

We are pushed to accept leaders that are perpetrators of sexual assault and malicious behavior; the adverse traumatic experiences that we already know fuel substance use. If recovery advocacy is truly a movement, it must part ways with the same political and economic systems that have already failed our addicted friends, family and community members for the last century. The recovery movement must have different representation at its town halls and forums as well; doing away with excessive cis-white panels and speakers as if colonizing, oppressive straight folk are the only people that recover and have experience worth sharing. Any real movement looking forward must be grassroots, focused on social consciousness and led by BIPOC, LGBTQ folx and women to ensure a moving away from and dismantling the systems of capitalism, white supremacy and patriarchy; the most prominent symptoms of the existing broken system.

If we understand from the basic recovery literature in the world's most popular programs that drinking and using drugs are a response to being restless or discomforted; why are we not doing everything we can to revolutionize the system to implement a society free from at least the unnecessary suffering? How are we not all supporting Medicaid/healthcare for all? We can and should implement and provide as many resources and funding as possible along the way, yet if we don't change the existing conditions under which people are motivated to use, we cannot get different results.

The wealthiest individuals and families in our nation continue to benefit off of the ongoing struggles in our communities, from the top tiers of Big Pharma and the Sackler family, to those who run for-profit prison systems, as well as the corporations that keep us in bondage to low wages, leeching off of our labor; paying into their healthcare plans and keeping us disconnected.

Many of us live dysfunctional lives at home, working just to make ends meet for another month. Our most morally bankrupt politicians are lobbied with millions of dollars to try and ensure what works for them in financial prestige and power doesn't go away. These are the mechanisms that ensure addiction thrives and the aim is to keep it that way; but there could be less dependence on drugs and alcohol if there were an ability to be dependent on a more socially focused, equitable system. This current system does not want us to know the true value of our labor, communities, or for us to experience our own resiliency and innate ability to overcome adversities such as drug addiction. We have to change the entire system. Again, nothing changes if nothing changes.

Once again harm reduction practices, medication to treat substance use and supporting moderation are all absolutely necessary and essential in the path forward. People need relief from life lived in this American society. For recent examples, one only needs to look at the impact of American history and racism on communities of color; or the impact that the opioid epidemic has had on states like West Virginia, Ohio and many more over the last two decades; how industrial jobs and the sense of making a living disappeared and addiction took flight, seemingly overnight. Until society and the people in it no longer find it necessary to escape its harshest realities, we need to believe in and support paths that don't only involve complete abstinence. Twelve step, abstinence-based programs began at a time when the American household could get by on far less of an income without both adults working forty plus hours a week. The times have changed, increasingly towards being more difficult, and we know bootstrapping is a myth that favors the already privileged in our society. Hence, abstinence based recovery can't and won't always be the goal because we haven't undone the structures that keep suffering and/or recovering addicts from equitable, affordable or accessible healthcare, housing, and employment. Also, once and for all clearing away paralyzing drug conviction records, restoring voting rights and nurturing healthy reintegration back into society. But what's the use if one returns to that same society; the one that has continuously failed and stigmatized them because of the war on drugs and traumas inflicted by an ongoing capitalist system? We have to support larger, longer lasting, profound socioeconomic changes and radically compassionate drug policy rather than settle for more of the same capitalist rubbish.

Currently, everything has a price on it with an intent to profit. Your and my addiction and trauma has become a free market free for all that has ended up with insurance companies and individuals body brokering us into bogus treatment centers and for-profit, so-called justice systems; ultimately keeping many of us in a recovery class-war between abstinence and harm reduction, this path or that path, either approving or holding disdain for someone's way out of the bottomless hell of potentially fatal substance use. Until we introduce and instill a model that says we won't settle for the continuous incarceration and criminalizing of substance using populations, we will be mandated to hold abstinence in high regard since the criminal legal system depends upon that model, often forcing many who are system-involved to attend only abstinence-based mutual support groups like twelve step, where shame and alienation do exist for those who cannot stop using. The existing criminal legal system cannot fully concede in empathy to reducing harm when it is the most consistent purveyor of harm in our society.

The road ahead toward effective decriminalization and legalization will require a safer supply of narcotics, focusing on overall drug user health, and will take years and perseverance. It will also continue to take the blood, sweat and tears of our families and community members. In the meantime, since it will be difficult to eradicate the current oppressive system, as much as it should remain the goal we will not eradicate addiction. This is just the truth of our situation. Our goal along the way should be to practice tolerance; learning to live with the realities of addiction, walking alongside it and showing up compassionately for our community members. Understand that we will lose loved ones; that we will carry grief and our hearts will often hurt and break along the way. But we can also experience freedom, recovery and healing if we continue to fight and get behind true, socially conscious change.

Acknowledgements

It's important to begin by acknowledging that the writing of this book and many of the most valuable experiences in it have occurred on the unceded ancestral lands of the first people of Seattle, the Duwamish People, past and present.

In sincere gratitude for every experience I have ever endured, I could go on for days naming off individuals and organizations who have contributed to my life and events that have come to shape this book, but I will try to keep it to those that have been of unwavering support throughout my addiction, and even more so as I made my way into recovery. I'll also point out that I've been supported by many incredible womxn throughout my life. I'd like to begin by thanking my spouse April, who has been supportive for the countless hours that turned into days as I poured my heart and experiences into these pages; your encouragement, love and insight has moved me further in this journey than I could have ever imagined; I love you! My cousin Cheryl, for being the first to read the book and pushing me to get this out into the world. The support of my colleagues and team at King County Drug Diversion Court who began not so long ago as the team initially working twice as hard as me to save my life. Chelsea Baylen and Mary Taylor for consistently believing in me and bringing my voice of lived experience to various tables. Shannon Thomas for our conversations and your questions which continued to reshape and refine my personal perspectives. My dear friends Amy Mahaney and Chris Senecal for never once giving up on me, even in my darkest times. Seiho Morris, Kevin Ronca, and Wesley Irwin for taking this book for an early spin and sharing your thoughts and words in support of this work.

My sangha with Refuge Recovery and Rebel Saints Meditation Society. Noah Levine for your ongoing support of my journey and writing your memoir that changed my life over the course of two afternoons in a jail cell. Sean Fargo for guiding me in deepening my mindfulness practice and the ability to carry that to others that would benefit. My yoga teachers and community beginning with Kathleen Hunt and John Wilson; Jess Frank and the staff at Yoga Behind Bars. The Twelve Step community at Cherry Fellowship Hall; more specifically Brad C, Yvonne A, Marianne M, Mike C, Amir I, Ben H and Michael R; and the wisdom, energy and effort of Phil L in my first year of recovery.

The following agencies, people and organizations have either helped me establish my recovery or have offered me the opportunity to attend trainings/give back: Killian Noe, Ruby Takushi and staff at Recovery Café; Seth Welch and the students at the Recovery High School in Queen Anne; King County Behavioral Health and Recovery Division; Washington Recovery Alliance/King County Recovery Coalition; Ryan Hampton, Garrett Hade and the entire Mobilize Recovery family. Philip Jones and Nicquelle Jones with Therapeutic Health Services; Choose 180; Ryan Mielcarek and the Veteran Rites community.

To my mother; even during the most difficult times I know

you just wanted me to be free from suffering; I've finally found a way and I appreciate your love and kindness. To my brothers and sisters: thank you for lifting up my journey in recovery and your ongoing support. My cousins and family in western Massachusetts for believing in my ability to finally change the way I lived. To my child's mother, R: my deepest gratitude for your taking care of our child when I didn't have the wherewithal to show up as a parent and partner; you endured more than most at the hands of my addiction, and I'm just grateful we found recovery for the benefit of Ione and our true selves; also to your family for supporting my child, her mother and my recovery journey; the last five years would not have been possible without your help.

Lastly, to my daughter Ione: every one of these aforementioned individuals and organizations have given me the greatest gift ever; the ability and tools to be in your life. I appreciate your patience with me as a human and father, and have greatly appreciated your enthusiasm and support for me as I've written this memoir; I love you so much.

Joe Conniff is a person living in long-term recovery. Born and raised in Agawam, Massachusetts, he spent sixteen years in active drug addiction, ultimately compromising his military career, relationships and personal well-being along the way. He has been in recovery for over five years and is currently a peer counselor, mindfulness teacher, and recovery advocate. He lives in Seattle, Washington with his spouse and daughter.